MINNESOTA DAY TRIPS
BY THEME

BY MARY M. BAUER

Adventure Publications, Inc.
Cambridge, MN

Dedication

To Kenny, Rob, and Shelly—the loves of my life.

About the Author

A full-blooded Irish lass, Mary M. Bauer was born and raised in Lutefisk Country. She and her husband jumped the state line over a dozen years ago and bought a Wisconsin dairy farm. Her two children ran off to college, then found careers, to avoid baling hay and fence painting. A former nurse and interior designer, Mary began her writing career as a weekly columnist for a regional newspaper. She discovered ranting in public and getting paid for it is a lot of fun. She is the author of Adventure Publication's *Wisconsin Day Trips by Theme*. Besides family, her major loves are traveling, hiking, books, decrepit Christmas decorations, and Reese's Peanut Butter Cups. She is a dog and cat person, and is thinking about adopting a pig.

Book design by Jonathan Norberg

10 9 8 7 6

Copyright 2002 by Mary M. Bauer
Published by Adventure Publications, Inc.
820 Cleveland Street South
Cambridge, MN 55008
1-800-678-7006
www.adventurepublications.net
Printed in the United States of America
ISBN 13: 978-1-885061-99-7
ISBN 10: 1-885061-99-4

MINNESOTA
DAY TRIPS
BY THEME

INTRODUCTION / CONTENTS

So you want to tour Minnesota, and who wouldn't? After all, it is the birthplace of the mighty Mississippi River. It's also home to the world-renowned Mayo Clinic, the Mall of America, 3M and the childhood farm of American aviation hero Charles Lindbergh. Cheerleading, the black box and Spam™ are only a few of the creations invented in this land of 10,000 lakes. *National Geographic Magazine* states Minnesota's Boundary Waters Canoe Area Wilderness is "one of the 50 places everyone should visit during their lifetime." And no one should miss the spectacular fall colors as the leaves turn from lush summer greens to brilliant reds and golds.

Minnesota Day Trips takes the information overload out of planning an excursion. Each chapter offers a number of attractions based on themes such as train trips, family days, romantic getaways, waterfalls and so on. Simply turn to the chapters that appeal and bypass the rest if you'd like.

For an overview of Minneapolis and St. Paul, take the 3½-hour guided tour offered by metroConnections. From a deluxe motor coach, you'll see the Skyway system, Metrodome, Historic Fort Snelling, State Capitol, Guthrie Theater, lovely Summit Avenue, residential areas and many more interesting sights. Call metroConnections at 612-333-TOUR (8687) or 800-747-TOUR; www.metroconnections.com

Minneapolis has a Light Rail system linking the Downtown with the airport and the Mall of America. Fares range from .50 cents to $2.75. Children ages 5 and under are free with paid adult. Trains run daily from 4 a.m.– 1 a.m. Purchase tickets at vending machines located on station platforms. For more information call 800-NEW-RIDER or 612-373-3333; www.metrotransit.org/rail

For more information about the Twin Cities, contact:

Minneapolis Chamber of Commerce, 81 S 9th St, Ste 200, Minneapolis; 612-370-9100; www.minneapolischamber.org

The Greater Minneapolis Convention & Visitors Bureau, 250 Marquette Ave S, Ste 1300, Minneapolis; 888-676-MPLS (888-676-6757); www.minneapolis.org

St. Paul Chamber of Commerce, 401 N Robert St, Ste 150, St. Paul; 651-223-5000; www.saintpaulchamber.com

St. Paul Convention and Visitors Bureau, 175 W Kellogg Blvd, St. Paul; 1-800-627-6101 or 651-265-4900; www.stpaulcvb.org

For information about greater Minnesota, contact the Minnesota Office of Tourism at 651-296-5029 or 800-657-3700; www.exploreminnesota.com

Many attractions within *Minnesota Day Trips* include options of nearby things to see and do. There is also a select number of Western Wisconsin getaways.

The "$" icon denotes lodging rates and meal prices:

Lodging

$	$50 and under
$$	$100 and under
$$$	$150 and under
$$$$	$200 and under
$$$$ + $	Over $200

Meals

$	$10 and under
$$	$20 and under
$$$	$30 and under
$$$$	$40 and under

So go ahead and attend a Lion's Club pancake breakfast, or have yourself a heaping helping of hotdish at a church supper. Tour Minnesota's many museums and art galleries, hike the North Country or fish the River Valley's clear trout streams. Enjoy the land and that good old Midwestern friendliness Minnesotans are famous for.

Contents

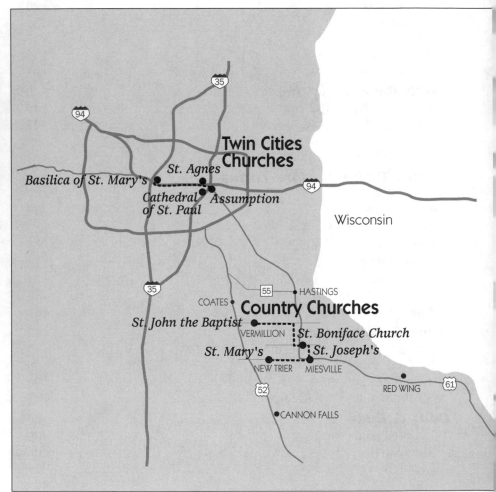

Twin Cities Churches

Basilica of St. Mary's

St. Agnes

Cathedral of St. Paul

Assumption

Wisconsin

HASTINGS

COATES

Country Churches

St. John the Baptist

VERMILLION

St. Boniface Church

St. Mary's

St. Joseph's

NEW TRIER

MIESVILLE

RED WING

CANNON FALLS

THEME: **CHURCHES**

Twin Cities Churches

Country Churches

CHURCHES
MINNESOTA
3:16

*C*hurches function as gathering places for those of like beliefs. The buildings are as diverse as the people they serve.

This chapter offers tours of Catholic churches rich in history and steeped in tradition—right down to the stained glass windows and pungent scent of burning incense. Marvel at the exquisitely crafted pews and confessionals, hand-painted statues and stenciled ceilings and walls. Domed naves arch to the heavens.

Most churches are open daily—usually until early evening. Use a side entrance if you find the front doors locked.

Twin Cities Churches

Cathedral of St. Paul

239 Selby Ave, St. Paul (across from the Minnesota History Center); 651-228-1766; www.cathedralsp.org

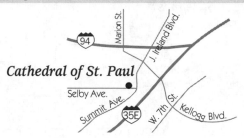

Cathedrals need not be grand—the only requirement is that they house the bishop's chair or *cathedra*. However, the Cathedral of St. Paul is regally grand, serving the Archdiocese of St. Paul and Minneapolis. French architect Emmanuel Louis Masqueray produced the cathedral's modified Renaissance design in the early 1900s (Masqueray also designed the basilica). Behind the massive altar, separate alcoves display hauntingly beautiful statues of several patron saints. Wheelchair accessible.

Assumption

51 W 7th St, downtown St. Paul; 651-224-7536

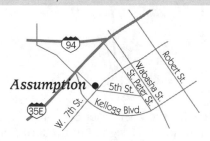

Assumption Church boasts twin steeples and beautifully manicured grounds. Wheelchair accessible.

Option: Don't miss your chance for some tasty Mulligan stew at **Mickey's Diner**, located directly across the street from Assumption Church on the corner of St. Peter and 7th Streets. The red-and-yellow streetcar building is one of only two diners in the country listed on the National Register of Historic Places. In business 24 hours a day, seven days a week since 1939, Mickey's long list of satisfied customers includes actors Bill Murray and Arnold Schwarzenegger—$.

St. Agnes

548 Lafond Ave, St. Paul (from the State Capitol, take University Ave west to Dale St, turn north, 5 blocks down turn east onto Lafond Ave, go 1 block); 651-293-1710; www.stagnes.net

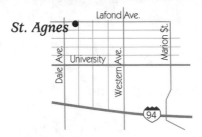

This gorgeous 1912 German church with its crystal chandeliers and marble columns still offers Solemn Mass, complete with Latin chants every Sunday at 10 a.m. Confessions may be heard in the German language, if the need arises. Wheelchair accessible.

Basilica of St. Mary's

88 N 17th St, Minneapolis (along I-94, across from Loring Park); 612-333-1381; www.mary.org

Built in the early 1900s, the Basilica of St. Mary's is every bit as impressive as those found in Rome. Designed in modern Renaissance style with a Byzantine treatment of the dome—that is, the church has a massive, lantern-crowned dome lifted from the substructure. The ceiling in the nave is 75' high and made of carved ornamental plaster. The stained glass windows depict the life of the Virgin Mary, to whom the basilica is dedicated. Wheelchair accessible.

Options: Pull up a park bench in nearby **Loring Park** for some great people watching, or take a leisurely stroll through the colorful gardens. Tour the many interesting cafes and boutiques in the area, then walk across the foot bridge to explore the 10-acre **Minneapolis Sculpture Garden**.

Country Churches

St. John the Baptist

106 W Main St, Vermillion, MN; 651-437-5652

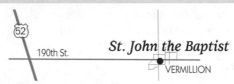

This 1913 church has wonderful fluted columns, a half-circle choir loft, more than a dozen stained glass windows, a domed ceiling and ornate plaster moldings. A glorious trek into the past. Wheelchair accessible.

St. Boniface Church

21889 Michael Ave, Hastings, MN; 651-437-2693; www.littleloghouseshow.com

Originally located in Hastings, historic St. Boniface found itself slated for demolition in 1995. Steve and Sylvia Bauer, owners of the Little Log House Village and Antique Power Show, bought the 1892 German Catholic church and dismantled it brick by brick, preserving the limestone foundation as well. They moved the materials, including the original stained glass windows, woodwork, light fixtures, pews and white painted altar to their antique village, then rebuilt the church ⅔ scale. Open only during Little Log House Antique Power Show in last full F, Sa, Su in July. Fee charged. Wheelchair accessible.

> **Option:** Established in 1989, the Bauer's privately owned **Little Log House Village** comes alive annually during the last full weekend in July. See antique tractors work the fields as the threshers harvest grain. Belly up to the bar at the once bustling saloon, or watch the miller grind flour using water wheel power. Explore old homesteads, an operating sawmill,

a blacksmith shop, a general store, a school house, a butcher shop, a brothel, the Soo Line Depot and train, and old cars, machinery and tools. Stroll more than 40,000 sq. ft. of beautiful gardens that were featured in the September 1999 issue of *Country Living* magazine. Take a walk or buggy ride across the world-famous spiral bridge (one of only three known to have existed in the world). Concessions; fee charged.

NOTE: Although the public may not enter the grounds without permission during the rest of the year, the village is definitely worth a drive by.

St. Joseph's

23955 Nicolai Ave, Hastings, MN; 651-437-3526

Constructed in 1906, St. Joseph's was completely rebuilt after a devastating fire. Tradition is alive and evident in this village church, right down to the unmistakable aroma of incense and candles burning before patron saints. St. Joe's also has beautifully carved confessionals, wall stencils, hand-painted statues and a half dozen beautiful stained glass windows—including one in the balcony. Wheelchair accessible.

St. Mary's

8433 239th St E, New Trier, MN; 651-437-5520

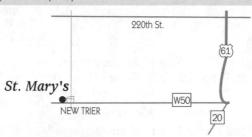

St. Mary's is an imposing structure of red and white brick built high on a hill overlooking New Trier, a small village of 96 souls. The 1909 church is on the National Register of Historic Places and boasts an annual sausage supper right along with its mass schedule. Marvel at the unique curved communal rail, altar and side altars—all constructed of dark butternut edged in gold. The church has a domed ceiling over the nave and more than a dozen stained glass windows. Wheelchair accessible.

St. Mary's

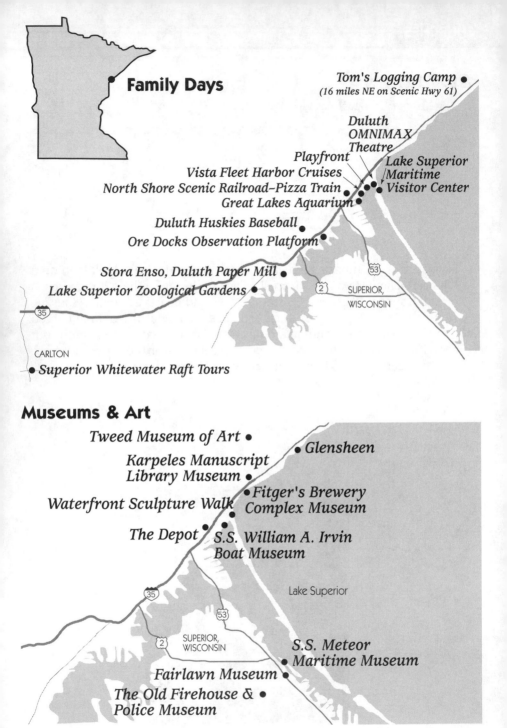

Family Days

Tom's Logging Camp •
(16 miles NE on Scenic Hwy 61)

Duluth
OMNIMAX
Theatre
Playfront • *Lake Superior*
Vista Fleet Harbor Cruises • *Maritime*
North Shore Scenic Railroad–Pizza Train • *Visitor Center*
Great Lakes Aquarium •
Duluth Huskies Baseball •
Ore Docks Observation Platform •

Stora Enso, Duluth Paper Mill •
Lake Superior Zoological Gardens •

SUPERIOR,
WISCONSIN

CARLTON
• *Superior Whitewater Raft Tours*

Museums & Art

Tweed Museum of Art •
• *Glensheen*
Karpeles Manuscript
Library Museum •
• *Fitger's Brewery*
Waterfront Sculpture Walk • *Complex Museum*
The Depot • *S.S. William A. Irvin*
Boat Museum

Lake Superior

SUPERIOR,
WISCONSIN
S.S. Meteor
• *Maritime Museum*
Fairlawn Museum •
The Old Firehouse & •
Police Museum

THEME: DULUTH

Family Days

Museums & Art

Duluth
NEXT LEFT

Romantic Getaways

The Mansion

Olcott House B&B

Leif Erikson Park

Greenery/Bridgeman's

Renegade Comedy Theatre

Radisson Hotel Duluth—Harborview

North Shore Scenic Railroad

Fitger's Brewery Complex

Bay Front Carriages

Vista Fleet Harbor Cruises

Skyline
Parkway

Lake Superior

35

2

2

53

SUPERIOR,
WISCONSIN

Lake Superior &
Mississippi Railroad

Romantic Getaways

A harbor town with a population of nearly 86,000, Duluth offers tons of outdoor activities, art and museum tours, a zoo, train and boat rides, gardens and parks, America's only all-freshwater aquarium, live theater, a casino, great dining, shopping and so much more.

The twin ports of Duluth and Superior, Wisconsin, are the leading bulk-cargo ports on the Great Lakes–St. Lawrence Seaway. Lake Superior is the largest freshwater lake in the world and the final resting place for more than 350 ships, including the famous Edmund Fitzgerald. *To help you get the most out of your Duluth trip, this chapter breaks down into several themes. Enjoy!*

Duluth

Duluth is 150 miles (2½ hours) north of the Twin Cities on I-35. Duluth Convention and Visitors Bureau: 800-4-DULUTH (800-438-5884) or 218-722-4011; www.visitduluth.com.

Family Days

More than a shipping port or honeymoon retreat, Duluth is a great place for families. Kids and parents alike will love these fun and educational attractions.

Lake Superior Maritime Visitor Center

On the waterfront in Canal Park next to the Aerial Lift Bridge; 218-720-5260, ext. 1; www.lsmma.com

The Lake Superior Maritime Visitor Center features full-scale replicas of ship cabins, recovered artifacts from sunken ships, film presentations, sightseeing information and posted arrival and departure times of huge 1,000' freighters that pass within yards of the building. Open daily. Wheelchair accessible. Free.

NOTE: For more shipping information, call the Boatwatcher's Hotline 218-722-6489 (closed Feb to mid-Mar), or the Duluth Shipping News 218-722-3119; www.duluthshippingnews.com.

Vista Fleet Harbor Cruises

323 Harbor Dr; 218-722-6218 or 877-883-4002; www.vistafleet.com

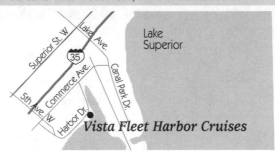

Vista Fleet Harbor Cruises

For a close-up view of a huge lake freighter, take a Vista Harbor Cruise. They offer an interesting, narrated 1½-hour tour of the harbor and information about the ships at port. Mid-May to mid-Oct. Wheelchair accessible. Fee charged.

NOTE: Vista Fleet also offers a variety of cruises which include meals. Call or check the website for more information.

Stora Enso, Duluth Paper Mill

100 N Central Ave.; 218-628-5100

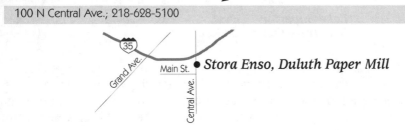

Stora Enso, Duluth Paper Mill

Ever wonder where paper comes from and how it's made? Tour this high-tech, world-class paper mill for all the answers. Must be at least 10 years of age, reservations required. Tours given Memorial Day–Labor Day, M, W, & F: Pick up tickets at the Vista Fleet dock office on Harbor Drive. Free.

Superior Whitewater Raft Tours

950 Chestnut Ave, Carlton, MN; 218-384-4637. Located 15 miles south of Duluth on the St. Louis River in Carlton; www.minnesotawhitewater.com

Does your family crave action-packed adventure? Then take them white-water rafting. Superior Whitewater Raft Tours supplies everything—equipment, shuttle service and guides—for a wet and wild two- to three-hour ride on the St. Louis River. No experience necessary, but must be age 12 or older. Daily May–Sep. Fee charged.

Option: Jay Cooke State Park, 500 E Hwy 210, Carlton, MN; 218-384-4610 (eastern edge of town). More than 14 miles of scenic biking and hiking from Carlton to Duluth. The park's focal point is a swinging suspension bridge overlooking an awesome gorge. Keep in mind that the bike or hike back is uphill!

Ore Docks Observation Platform

Located at 35th Ave W and Superior St. Take I-35 south to the 40th Ave W exit; go left over freeway and take another left at the Mesabi Ore Dock.

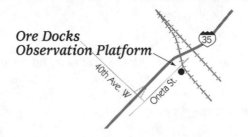

Railway docks extend more than 2,000' over the harbor. The observation platform offers an excellent view of the fascinating ship-loading operation. Free.

NOTE: Visitors must stay behind the guard shack.

North Shore Scenic Railroad—Pizza Train

The Depot (downtown Duluth), 506 W Michigan St; 218-722-1273
or 800-423-1273; www.northshorescenicrailroad.org

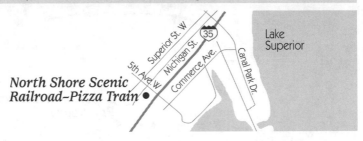

Enjoy a 2½-hour trip aboard a vintage train as it rumbles over tall trestles spanning deep river gorges, but you won't have to ride on an empty stomach. This adventure includes lots of Domino's Pizza and fun! Memorial Day–Labor Day, W–Sa: and F–Sa through October 15. Wheelchair accessible. Reservations required. Fee charged.—$$.

Duluth Huskies Baseball

Wade Stadium, 34th Ave W & Grand Ave; 218-786-9909; www.duluthhuskies.com

Take in a ball game at the historic Wade Stadium, home to the Duluth Huskies. The team plays over 50 regular season home games facing tough opponents like the St. Paul Saints. June–August. Wheelchair accessible. Call for season schedule and ticket prices.

Playfront

Bayfront Festival Park at the base of 5th Ave W (on the waterfront by the Great Lakes Aquarium).

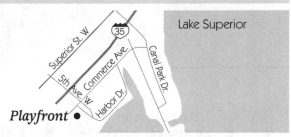

Take a picnic lunch to the Playfront at Bayfront Festival Park and let the kids run wild. They'll have a blast on all the cool playground equipment, giving you a chance to put your feet up and relax. By the way, you're in a perfect position for watching giant ore freighters cruise into the harbor.

Duluth OMNIMAX Theatre

301 Harbor Dr (on the waterfront next to the William A. Irvin); 218-727-0022; www.decc.org/attractions/omni.htm

Rainy day? No problem. See a show at the OMNIMAX Theatre. The mega-screen and advanced sound system make you feel like you're part of the action. Open daily. Wheelchair accessible. Fee charged.

NOTE: Separate fee charged for parking lot. Free parking spaces available within walking distance.

Lake Superior Zoological Gardens

7210 Fremont Street; 218-733-3777; www.lszoo.org

More than 25 endangered and threatened species from around the world live at the zoo, including Snow Leopards, Black-Footed Ferrets, Bald Eagles, Siberian Tigers, kangaroos and Polar Bears. Primate Conservation Center, gift shop and cafe. Open daily. Wheelchair accessible. Fee charged. Children 2 and under free.

Great Lakes Aquarium

353 Harbor Dr; 218-740-3474; www.glaquarium.org

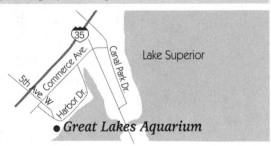

The Great Lakes Aquarium features a unique 120,000-gallon display. Captain an ore freighter and learn about the unpredictable weather patterns responsible for sinking ships. Experience over 30 interactive exhibits including glaciers, lava flows and wave creation. Otters, frogs, fish, birds and mammals throughout. Changing exhibits and special programs. Open Daily. Fee charged. Children 3 and under free.

NOTE: Separate fee for parking.

Tom's Logging Camp

5797 North Shore Dr (16 miles northeast of Duluth on scenic Hwy 61); 218-525-4120; www.tomsloggingcamp.com

At Tom's Logging Camp, you'll learn how the Minnesota loggers lived and worked before the chainsaw. Try your hand at blacksmithing or feed pygmy goats, bunnies and rainbow trout. Step inside the gravity house and watch a ball mysteriously roll uphill! Open daily May–Oct. Gift shop. Fee charged. Children age 5 and under free.

Aerial Lift Bridge, near the Lake Superior Maritime Visitor Center (pg. 19)

Museums & Art

From gorgeous works of art, to the world's only historic whaleback freighter, to murder—Duluth's museums have it all!

Glensheen

3300 London Rd (five miles east of downtown Duluth); 218-726-8910 or 888-454-GLEN (888-454-4536); www.d.umn.edu/glen

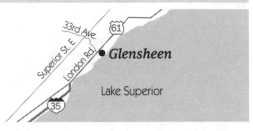

Listed on the National Register of Historic Places, this luxurious, 39-room Jacobean-style mansion completed in 1908 showcases custom-designed furnishings original to the house. In 1977, an upstairs bedroom was the scene of the brutal double murder of heiress Elisabeth Congdon and her nurse. Congdon's daughter and son-in-law were tried for the crime, and the son-in-law was found guilty.

Grounds include formal gardens, carriage house with carriage collection, gardener's cottage and clay tennis court. Tours conducted daily May–Oct, weekends Nov–April. Wheelchair accessible. Fee charged.

Tweed Museum of Art

University of Minnesota Duluth Campus, 1201 Ordean Court; 218-726-7823; www.d.umn.edu/tma

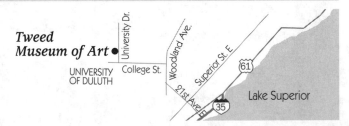

Contemporary and historical American and European art is displayed in the museum's nine galleries. Also featured is the Glenn C. Nelson International Ceramics Collection and the Potlatch "Mountie" Illustration Collection. The

museum hosts approximately ten exhibitions annually. Gift shop. Open Sa–Su. Wheelchair accessible. Donation suggested.

Karpeles Manuscript Library Museum

902 E 1st St; 218-728-0630; www.rain.org/~karpeles/dul.html

Established by California businessman and Duluth native, David Karpeles, the museum houses original handwritten drafts of the U.S. Bill of Rights, the Emancipation Proclamation Amendment, Handel's Messiah and many more important historical documents, maps from around the world. Sheet music from Mozart, Bach, Beethoven. Open Tu–Su (daily in summer).

Fitger's Brewery Complex Museum

600 E Superior St; 218-722-8826; www.fitgers.com

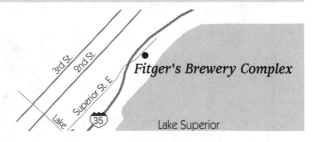

Fitger's is the longest continuously operating brewery in Minnesota. Established in 1857, it survived the Prohibition years by producing soda pop and candy bars. The museum specializes in northern Minnesota brewing history and memorabilia from what was once one of the most successful breweries in the state. Open daily. Wheelchair accessible. Free.

NOTE: Fitger's Brewhouse serves sandwiches, soups, burgers and has its own handcrafted ales on tap—$.

Waterfront Sculpture Walk

Canal Park—Lakeshore Walk

Waterfront Sculpture Walk

A series of sculptures representing the social, cultural and historical values of Duluth and cities around the world create an outdoor gallery of international art.

> **Option:** Have lunch at **Grandma's Restaurant** or, at least, take a peek inside at the interesting paraphernalia hanging from the ceiling and on the walls. Burgers, specialty sandwiches, Marathon Spaghetti, steak and more. Open daily. $–$$.

S.S. William A. Irvin Ore Boat Museum

350 Harbor Dr; 218-722-7876 or 218-722-5573 (Duluth Entertainment and Convention Center); www.williamairvin.com

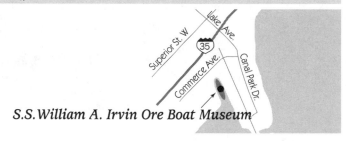

S.S. William A. Irvin Ore Boat Museum

A floating museum permanently docked across from the Duluth Entertainment Convention Center, the *William A. Irvin* was once the flagship of U.S. Steel's Great Lakes Fleet. It carried ore and coal for 40 years. One-hour guided tour of engine room, staterooms, galley, dining room and pilothouse. Open daily. Fee charged.

> **Option:** The last two weeks before Halloween, the stately *William A. Irvin* morphs into the **Ship of Ghouls**. The U of M Theatre Department offers haunted voyages into the unknown. But beware—this bone-chilling experience is not for the faint of heart! Call the museum for ticket information.

The Depot

506 W Michigan St; 218-727-8025 or 888-733-5833; www.duluthdepot.org

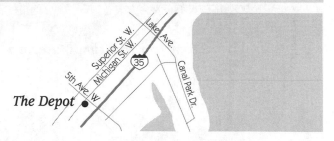

A must-see for every museum and art lover! Advertised as "everything under one roof," the 1892 Chateauesque-style Depot certainly has it all: Art Institute, Duluth Children's Museum, Lake Superior Railroad Museum, St. Louis County Historical Society, as well as the School of the Minnesota Ballet, Duluth Playhouse, Duluth-Superior Symphony Orchestra, Matinee Musicale and Arrowhead Chorale. Open daily. Wheelchair accessible. Fee charged. Ticket price includes admission to all four museums.

Fairlawn Museum

906 E 2nd St, Superior, WI (adjacent to Barker's Island); 715-394-5712; www.fairlawnmansion.org

Tour this 19th-century Victorian, 42-room house, which was once the home of lumber baron Martin Pattison. A 1998 renovation returned the house to its original splendor—carved wood, marble, silver trim, brass and English tile. Period-costumed tour guides. Open daily Memorial Day–Labor Day. Call for winter hours. Wheelchair accessible. Fee charged.

NOTE: Tour guides are not all the same—some are energetic, some are serious, but most are at least alive. Tourists have reported a very pleasant young servant gal guiding them through the museum Trouble is, the servant gal is a ghost!

S.S. Meteor Maritime Museum

Berthed on Barker's Island, WI; 715-392-2773 or 800-942-5313; www.fairlawnmansion.org/ssmeteor

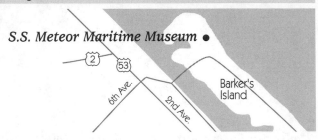

Launched in Superior in 1896, the S.S. Meteor is the world's only historic whaleback freighter still in existence. Daily tours mid-May–mid-Oct. Fee charged. Wheelchair accessible only on first floor.

The Old Firehouse & Police Museum

402 23rd Ave E (just south of Hwys 2 & 53), Superior, WI; 715-398-7558, 715-394-5712 or 800-942-5313; www.fairlawnmuseum.org/firehouse

3rd St.	The Old Firehouse & Police Museum		
4th St.		●	
5th St.	22nd Ave.	23rd Ave.	24th Ave.

The 1890s fire station houses vintage fire engines, a unique collection of toy fire engines, police and fire equipment, artifacts and the Wisconsin Fire and Police Hall of Fame. Mid-Mar–mid-Oct. Wheelchair accessible only on first floor. Free.

Romantic Getaways

Whether you've been together 50 years or are just starting out, Duluth is the place to go with the person you love.

Lake Superior & Mississippi Railroad

Train departs from 6930 Freemont St (at the hill across from the Lake Superior Zoo); 218-624-7549; www.lsmrr.org

Lake Superior & Mississippi Railroad

Begin your romantic getaway with an historic 90-minute journey along the scenic St. Louis River. The LS&M traces its roots back to 1863 and was the first railroad linking Duluth to the Twin Cities. Vintage equipment and open "Safari Car" excursions. Mid-Jun to Labor Day, Sa & Su: Fee charged.

Fitger's Brewery Complex

600 E Superior St; 218-279-BREW; www.brewhouse.net

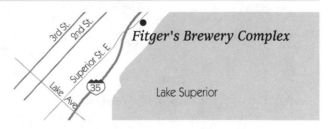

Fitger's Brewery Complex

Lake Superior

Fitger's was a brewery from 1885 until 1972. Now a shopping complex with elegant dining opportunities and an overnight guest inn, learn about its history in the free museum. **Fitger's Brewhouse Brewery & Grille** features its own award-winning handcrafted ales, homemade soups, sandwiches, burgers and more. Wheelchair accessible—$.

Options: Stop by **Wine Cellars, Inc.** (within the Fitger's complex) and choose a favorite wine from their more than 1,000 vintages. • Fifty cents gets you a ride on the **Port Town Trolley** from the Waterfront to Fitger's. Wheelchair accessible.

Olcott House Bed & Breakfast Inn

2316 E 1st St; 800-715-1339 or 218-728-1339; www.olcotthouse.com. Also see www.visitduluth.com/historicinns for more information on Duluth's historic bed & breakfast inns.

A 1904 "Gone With the Wind" historic grand mansion, the Olcott House offers a choice of six romantic suites with working fireplaces and private baths or a carriage house hideaway complete with kitchen and living room. Sip a glass of iced tea on the Grand Porch before going out for dinner or stroll the manicured grounds in the company of your sweetheart. Wonderful candlelight breakfast (fruit plate, wild rice omelet, meat, potato, coffee, tea, juice) or continental breakfast served in your suite—$$$.

Radisson Hotel Duluth—Harborview

505 W Superior St; 800-333-3333 or 218-727-8981; www.duluth.com/radisson

Make dinner reservations at Radisson's **Top of the Harbor**. Located on the 16th floor, the revolving restaurant offers a spectacular harbor and city view. Full revolution every 72 minutes. American cuisine. Wheelchair accessible. Dinner served daily. $–$$$.

Bay Front Carriages

4447 Caribou Lake Rd, Canal Park; 715-398-7386

Take a romantic carriage ride along the waterfront. Bay Front Carriages (across from Grandma's Restaurant) offers their horse-drawn service daily Jun–Aug; weekends only May, Sep, Oct. (weather permitting). Fee charged.

Leif Erikson Park & The Greenery/Bridgeman's

Leif Erikson Park is north of Fitger's Complex on London Rd.
The Greenery/Bridgeman's, Holiday Ctr, 1st Level, 200 W 1st St; 218-727-3387.

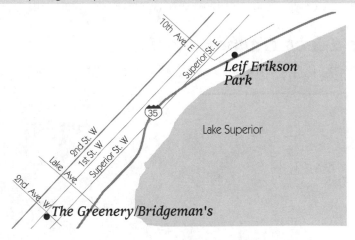

Order a picnic-to-go from the Greenery/Bridgeman's and head to the Rose Garden at Leif Erikson Park. One of Minnesota's prettiest parks, featuring more than 3,000 rosebushes, a fountain, a marble gazebo, an herb garden and plenty of comfortable benches overlooking the lake.

NOTE: Rose-blooming season begins in late June to early July.

Skyline Parkway

Take Hwy 53 north off of I-35. Skyline Parkway crosses Hwy 53

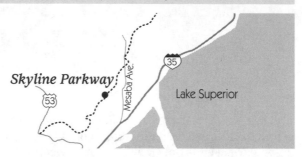

This dramatic, 30-mile drive 600' above the shoreline is one long, breathtaking view of Lake Superior and the harbor.

Options: There are frequent observation points and markers, including the tower at **Enger Park**. Seven Bridges Road winds through forested hillsides and over seven stone bridges. Explore caverns, waterfalls and the **Hawk Ridge Nature Reserve**, which is rated one of the nation's top ten viewing spots for hawks. www.hawkridge.org.

Vista Fleet Harbor Cruises

323 Harbor Dr; 218-722-6218 or 877-883-4002; www.vistafleet.com

Enjoy scenic Lake Superior and the international harbor aboard the Vista Star. The 2-hour dinner cruise serves prime rib and chicken. Wheelchair accessible. Call for hours. Reservations required—$$$$.

North Shore Scenic Railroad

The Depot, 506 W Michigan St; 800-423-1273 or 218-722-1273;
www.northshorescenicrailroad.org

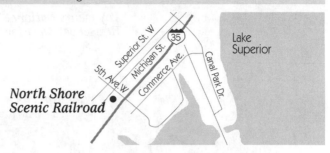

The North Shore Scenic Railroad offers a special 2½-hour Elegant Dinner Train excursion hosted by various Duluth restaurants. Restored vintage train rumbles through the city along the rugged shoreline and deep into the North Woods. Trip scheduled for selected weekends only. Limited wheelchair accessibility. Call ahead for reservations, menu and dates. $$$$ + $.

Renegade Comedy Theatre

222 E Superior St; 218-336-1414 or 888-722-6627;
www.renegadecomedytheatre.com

Top off your evening with a show like you've never seen before! Renegade is the only professional theater company in the Northland devoted exclusively to fun and laughs. It offers original comedy revues and comic productions by established playwrights such as Durang, Kling & Simon. A megahit is the nightly Renegade Improv Comedy Olympics: two teams of improvisational comedians compete for points and laughter in scene games based on audience suggestions. Saturday nights only. Call for reservations and ticket prices.

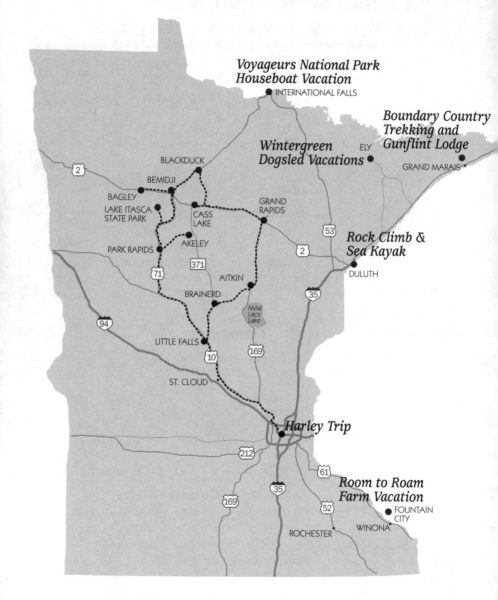

Voyageurs National Park
Houseboat Vacation
● INTERNATIONAL FALLS

Boundary Country
Trekking and
Gunflint Lodge

Wintergreen
Dogsled Vacations   ELY ●

GRAND MARAIS ●

BLACKDUCK

BEMIDJI

BAGLEY

LAKE ITASCA
STATE PARK

CASS
LAKE

GRAND
RAPIDS

(2)

(53)

Rock Climb &
Sea Kayak

PARK RAPIDS   AKELEY

(2)

(71)   371

AITKIN

DULUTH

BRAINERD

Mille
Lacs
Lake

(35)

(94)

LITTLE FALLS

(10)   (169)

ST. CLOUD

Harley Trip

(212)

(61)

Room to Roam
Farm Vacation

(169)   (35)

(52)   ● FOUNTAIN
CITY

ROCHESTER   WINONA

THEME: *EXTREME ADVENTURES*

*M*innesota's diverse landscapes and ever changing seasons are not only breathtakingly beautiful, but provide great opportunities for the adventure seeker as well.

For all of you who hunger for a different kind of a vacation—one that caters to your free spirit—this chapter is for you. From dairy farming, to mushing a dog team, to renting a houseboat, Minnesota is your vacationland for adventure!

Voyageurs National Park Houseboats

Voyageurs National Park; Approximately 300 miles north of the Twin Cities, about a 5-hour drive. www.nps.gov/voya/

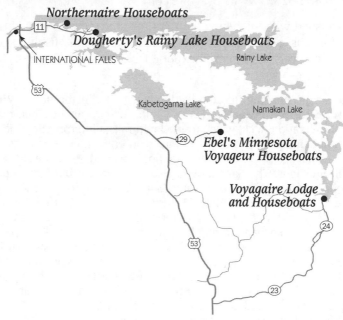

Do you want to get away from it all? Then head to Voyageurs National Park. The least used of all national parks, Voyageurs is definitely north of "up north," sharing a common boundary with Canada. More than 500 islands and over 30 lakes establishes it as the park with the most water. At 2.7 billion years old, Voyageurs' plentiful, gray-colored Canadian Shield is among the oldest rock in the world. Hunt, fish, canoe or pick blueberries to your heart's content. Visit old gold mines, a primitive sculpture garden or the historic Kettle Falls Hotel—reported as haunted! Hike trails to waterfalls, island hop or skinny-dip (if you're so inclined), because it's only you and miles of scenic, untamed nature.

There are four points of entry into Voyageurs besides International Falls: Crane Lake, Ash River, Lake Kabetogama and Rainy Lake. The following is a list of local houseboat rental firms:

- Dougherty's Rainy Lake Houseboats: 2031 Town Rd 488, International Falls, MN 56649; 800-554-9188 or 218-286-5391; www.rainylakehouseboats.com.

- Ebel's Minnesota Voyageur Houseboats: 10326 Ash River Tr, Orr, MN 55771; 888-883-2357 or 218-374-3571; www.ebels.com.

- Northernaire Houseboats: 2690 Co 94, International Falls, MN 56649; 800-854-7958; www.northernairehouseboats.com.

- Voyagaire Lodge and Houseboats: 7576 Goldcoast Road, Crane Lake, MN 55725; 800-882-6287; www.voyagaire.com.

Boats are furnished with kitchen equipment, dishes and bedding. Linens, towels and hot tubs available for rent. Some firms include fishing boats. Extensive instructions given to inexperienced boaters. Season: Mid-May–mid-Oct. Rates vary.

Options: Before heading into the wilderness, make a stop at the **Vince Shute Wildlife Sanctuary** to learn a thing or two about black bears. From an observation deck, watch trained naturalists interpret bear behavior as it happens. But a word of caution—you enter the grounds at your own risk. Bears are wild animals and are not fenced in. Read the signs and follow all directions. The Sanctuary is also excellent for birding, so don't forget your binoculars! The Vince Shute Wildlife Sanctuary is 1 mile south of Orr on Pelican Lake. From Hwy 53, turn west on Co 23; drive 13 miles, sanctuary is on the right. Open Memorial Day–Labor Day, 5 p.m. until dusk. Closed Mondays and during heavy rainfall. Fee charged. No pets or motorcycles, as they scare the bears. For tour information, call 218-757-0172; www.americanbear.org. NOTE: The road cannot accommodate RVs or trailers over 26' long. • The **Orr Wetlands Walk** is a half-mile jaunt with wildlife and pelicans galore! Boardwalk begins at the Information Center parking lot located just south of Orr on Hwy 53. Call 800-357-9255 for naturalist-led tour times. Wheelchair accessible.

Wintergreen Dogsled Vacations

1101 Ring Rock Rd, Ely, MN 55731; 218-365-6022; www.dogsledding.com. Approximately 260 miles from the Twin Cities, about a 5-hour drive. NOTE: Flying in? Numerous 45-minute trips offered daily from the Twin Cities to Hibbing's full-service airport. Take the Ely Taxi for a 70-mile shuttle to the resort.

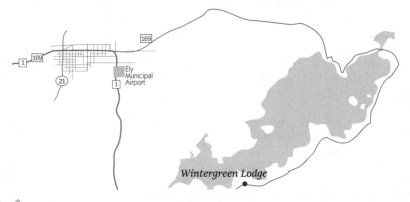

Wintergreen Lodge

In 1986, Paul Schurke and Will Steger successfully completed an amazing 57-day journey to the North Pole. Their success launched them new careers as best-selling authors and speakers with an award-winning television special. *Outside Magazine* named Paul the Outdoorsman of the Year. This vacation gives you a chance to go exploring with real-life Arctic adventurer Paul Schurke. For the past couple of decades, Paul has conducted complete hands-on mushing tours from his Wintergreen Lodge on White Iron Lake.

Wintergreen provides gear, food and lodging. If you don't know what to wear, Paul's wife, Sue, can hook you up with fleece anoraks or pants or whatever you need to keep toasty warm. Sue Schurke is the owner of Wintergreen Design, a specialty outdoor apparel manufacturer/retail store and catalog. Sue sewed all the clothing for Paul's 1986 North Pole expedition, launching her extremely successful business from the kitchen table. Rent or buy the clothing at a special guest discount.

Wintergreen has the world's largest working kennel of Canadian Eskimo freight dogs. The dogs range from 60–80 pounds and can pull twice their weight. And just because this is a wilderness adventure, don't think you'll be suffering in the food department. Wintergreen has a Cordon Bleu-certified French chef on staff. The Schurke family lives nearby on the grounds and often eats with the guests. Paul takes time to personally visit with the guests and share his Arctic adventures.

Physical requirements vary for each trip, with a recommended age of 8 years or older. Group size is 6–8. Book in advance, as trips fill by November. Call or check the website for trip package information.

Boundary Country Trekking (Yurt to Yurt!)

11 Poplar Creek Dr, Grand Marais, MN 55604; 800-322-8327 or 218-388-4487; www.boundarycountry.com. Grand Marais is approximately 260 miles from the Twin Cities. NOTE: The Gunflint Trail is one of two entrances into the Boundary Waters Canoe Area Wilderness.

Advertised as "civilized adventures for the active traveler," Boundary Country Trekking is on the Gunflint Trail. They offer a variety of vacation packages for every season including dogsledding, mountain biking, guided BWCAW canoe trips, and lodge to lodge hiking trips on the Superior

Hiking Trail. A popular winter trip is yurt to yurt skiing. (A yurt is a canvas-covered Mongolian hut with a round peaked roof.) If you're into building muscles and sweat, sign up for a Work Weekend of clearing the Banadad Ski Trail of downed trees and brush. The trail is within the BWCAW where power tools are not permitted, so all maintenance is done by hand labor. Lodging, meals and tools are provided. For more information on all Boundary Country Trekking's vacation options, check out their website or give them a call. $$–$$$$ + $.

NOTE: The **Boundary Waters Canoe Area Wilderness** (BWCAW) covers approximately 1 million acres and is the world's largest waterway wilderness. *National Geographic Magazine* claims it's "one of 50 places everyone should visit in their lifetime." You must have a BWCAW permit to enter, and motorized or mechanized vehicles of any kind are prohibited (snowmobiles, mountain bikes, etc.). They also have a strict "leave no trace" policy. For more info on the BWCAW or to obtain a permit, log on to www.bwcaw.org or call 877-550-6777.

Gunflint Lodge

143 S Gunflint Lake, Grand Marais, MN 55604; 800-328-3325 or 218-388-2294; www.gunflint.com. Lodge located 43 miles northwest on Gunflint Trail (Co 12).

There's no better way to "rough it" in the wilderness than to book a stay at the Gunflint Lodge. This third-generation, family-owned lodge features wood paneling, a stone fireplace and a gourmet chef who prepares sumptuous meals, such as grilled Atlantic Salmon with Ancho Maple Glaze and roasted stuffed Rainbow Trout Provençal. Their motto is: Arrive as a guest, and leave as a friend. A full friend, at that!

Feel like horseback riding through one of the most picturesque places on earth? Gunflint Lodge offers 1- and 2-hour trail rides through the Superior National Forest. Other riding packages include breakfast or dinner feasts prepared for you along the trail. The 27 cabins on Gunflint Lake range from 1–4 bedrooms. Most have indoor whirlpool baths and kitchens; several come equipped with a large outdoor whirlpool. All have living room fireplaces.

Gunflint Lodge specializes in "theme" vacations and retreats, such as mother and daughter weekends, lifestyle retreats, women's packages, fishing, canoeing, horseback riding, dogsledding and cross-country skiing. On-staff naturalist. Pets allowed. Special rates for off-season. Check website for dates and prices. $$$$ + $.

Rock Climb & Sea Kayak

The University of Minnesota Duluth; 218-726-7128; www.d.umn.edu/recreation. Duluth is approximately 150 miles north of the Twin Cities on I-35. The actual site of the trips vary, so call ahead for locations.

Have you always wanted to learn how to kayak or rock climb? The University of Minnesota Duluth offers several options for learning these skills, including safety and rescue clinics. Take an introductory course at Split Rock Lighthouse State Park kayaking the open waters of Lake Superior or paddle next to anchored ocean freighters on Duluth Waterfront Tours. Rock climb on the North Shore and enjoy nature's beauty. Half- or full-day courses. Prices range from $35–$100.

Once you've mastered the courses, sign up for the University's adventure trips. There are several to choose from throughout the summer and they change from year to year. Some examples include:

- Mountain bike and rock climb in the Moab desert. Cycle through sandstone landscapes and stand on ancient rock spires.

- Sea kayak the Brooks Peninsula on Vancouver Island. Visit with a Checleset Band family living on an outer coast island. Observe puffins, sea otters and sea lions. Fish for rock cod or halibut and examine historical totems.

- Alpine climb in Rocky Mountain National Park. Attempt to take the summit at 14,225'.

- Hike and canoe the Ozarks at Buffalo National River.

Skill level of trips varies from beginner to intermediate. Call or visit the University's website for schedule and pricing.

Harley Trip to the Headwaters

Midwest Motorcycle Rental and Tours, 215 Washington Ave N; 612-338-5345; www.midwestmotorcycle.com. (Downtown Minneapolis in the heart of the Warehouse District.)

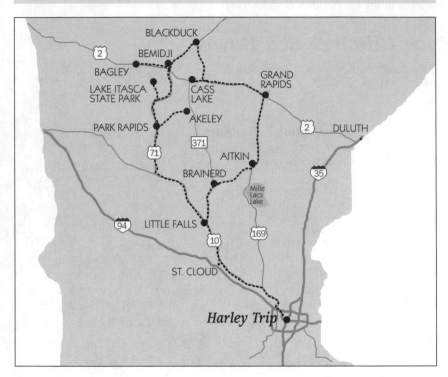

Who among us has not wanted to feel wild and completely free? Get away from the grind by renting a weekend of freedom at **Midwest Motorcycle Rental and Tours**. Straddle that powerful Harley and crank up the gas, because you're heading 200 miles north to the birthplace of something even more mighty than the beast between your legs: the Mississippi River in **Itasca State Park** (Minnesota's oldest state park). The main park entrance is 21 miles north of Park Rapids on Hwy 71. The Headwaters area is north and west of the east entrance off Park Drive.

It's at Itasca State Park that the Mississippi River begins her winding journey of more than 2,500 miles to the Gulf of Mexico. Stepping stones cross over her humble beginnings. Spend some time hiking the 33 miles of trails through a virgin pine forest that boasts the state's tallest Red Pine and White Pine. The park also has a new visitor center, gift shop, 100' fire tower you can climb and year-round programs including guided walks and boat tours. Bike, boat, canoe and snowshoe rental available. Reserve lodging and camping well in advance by calling the State Park Reservation System at 866-85PARKS (866-857-2757) or www.stayatmnparks.com.

While in the area, eat at the historic **Douglas Lodge** (218-266-2122), located near the park's east entrance. Decidedly Minnesotan, the menu includes such mainstays as wild rice soup and walleye. Wash down the meal with a nice bottle of wine—a Minnesota vintage, of course.

If you're looking for some evening entertainment, cruise on over to the **Woodtick Musical Jamboree** at the junction of Hwys 34 & 64 in downtown Akeley (roughly a 40-mile drive). Enjoy two lively hours of country, gospel and bluegrass music and comedy routines. Mid-Jun through mid-Sept, W–Sa: Fee charged. Call 800-644-6892 for reservations or 218-652-4200 for information, or visit www.woodticktheater.net.

Rise and shine with an all-you-can-eat lumberjack breakfast featuring stacks of pancakes, ham, eggs, hash browns, stewed prunes, juice, coffee and milk served family style on tin plates and cups at **Rapid River Logging Camp**. Elbow your way through the rustic dining hall and have a seat on a long pine picnic table. Afterward, visit the museum and stroll the nature trails. Steam-powered sawmill runs on Tu & F. Open daily Memorial Day through Labor Day 218-732-3444. Take Hwy 71 north of Park Rapids and follow the signs to Co 18.

Return to the Twin Cities via the **Great River Road** as it follows the Mississippi River between Itasca State Park and Little Falls. Travel the 200 miles through Bemidji, Grand Rapids, Aitkin and Brainerd. Watch for signs.

NOTE: With all of the thick hardwood forests, the Great River Road is also a designated route for viewing fall color.

> **Options:** If you have the time, head north of Itasca State Park to **Bemidji**. Have your picture taken next to 18' statues of Paul Bunyan and Babe, the Blue Ox, or any of the dozen sculptures along the waterfront. • **Lake Bemidji State Park** is 5 miles north of town on Co 21, then 2 miles east on Hwy 20, and worth your trip. You'll find naturalist programs, a boardwalk through a bog with insect-eating pitcher plants, miles of wooded trails and a swimming beach. The Showy Lady's Slipper (Minnesota's state flower) is in bloom from early Jun to early Jul. • The 32-mile **Scenic Byway Co 39** runs between Blackduck and Cass Lake. **Star Island** (accessible by boat only) sits smack dab in the middle of Cass Lake. The nearly 1,200-acre island is a mecca for Bald Eagles and boasts its own 195-acre lake, Lake Windigo—"the lake in the island in the lake." Say what? • The town of **Bagley** is west of Bemidji on Hwy 2. Its unusual wildlife museum showcases over 780 mounted specimens. You'll see it all here, from minnows to moose!

Room to Roam Farm Vacations

Room to Roam, W656 Veraguth Dr, Fountain City, WI 54629; 608-687-8575.
Approximately 120 miles south of the Twin Cities.

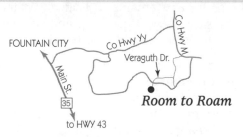

As a guest at the Room to Roam, a registered Holstein dairy farm, you can squirt milk at a cat, bottle-feed a newborn calf, gather fresh eggs and feed the cows—all before breakfast! Afterward, watch farmer Jess work up the fields, bale some hay or harvest the crops. Learn what it's like to be a farmer in this challenging global economy or just pet the animals and enjoy the peace and quiet.

The furnished 3-bedroom, century-old, two-story farmhouse sits high on the bluffs overlooking the mighty Mississippi River. You'll have your own big maple tree in the front yard and a garden ripe for the picking in the back. There's a volleyball setup, Schwan's vanilla ice cream in the freezer, a firepit with a supply of wood, hayrides and plenty of time for eagle watching (so bring your binoculars). Rent by the night, weekend, week or longer. The house sleeps eight comfortably. Rates: $100/night or $400/week.

NOTE: This is not a bed and breakfast. You are responsible for your own meals. The farmhouse is separate from the owners' house.

INTERNATIONAL FALLS

The Wild North
ELY

61

53

2

371

DULUTH

Minnesota
Legends

10

35

BRAINERD

94

LITTLE FALLS

169

ST. CLOUD

Kids' Museums

212

GRANITE
FALLS

Mall of America

Things That Fly

Lions, Tigers and Bears

Camp in a Real Tepee

169

35

Cannon River Tubing

Just Like Laura Ingalls Wilder

WALNUT
GROVE

SANBORN

WASECA

COMFREY

Farmamerica

71

52

Eagle Bluff Environmental
Learning Center

THEME: FAMILY DAY

The Wild North

Minnesota Legends

Kids' Museums

Things That Fly

Mall of America

Lions, Tigers and Bears

International Wolf Center (pg. 53)

*T*his chapter has the whole family in mind with attractions geared to entertain and educate. You'll find some outings are seasonal, while others may be a bit more tailored to certain ages. Pick the ones that are right for your gang and have fun!

The Wild North

Ely is approximately 255 miles north of the Twin Cities. Take I-35 north toward Duluth, then turn onto Hwy 33, which connects with Hwy 53. Follow 53 north to Hwy 169 east into Ely. Visit Ely's Chamber of Commerce online at www.ely.org.

International Wolf Center

1396 Hwy 169, Ely, MN; 800-ELY-WOLF (800-359-9653) or 218-365-4695, ext 21; www.wolf.org. Located at the far end of town.

You'll have a howling good time at the International Wolf Center. It features a guided evening trek into the heart of Minnesota's wolf country to explore the habitat of prey species such as beaver and white-tailed deer. The trek concludes with a howl to one of the local packs. Other programs offered include animal tracking hikes, a visit to a beaver lodge, and an opportunity for you to use radio telemetry—the latest device in tracking technology. Call for program schedules.

The Center also has its own resident wolves that are easily viewed from a window theater. Several times a day, naturalists introduce the pack and explain the basics of wolf biology, pack structure and communication. Interactive displays, gift shop, movies. May–mid-Oct, open daily; mid-Oct–Apr, open Sa–Su. Wheelchair accessible. Call for program schedules. Fee charged.

> **Option:** Visit the **Dorothy Molter Cabin Museum** located on Hwy 169 (next to the International Wolf Center). Molter was the last resident of the BWCAW. Each year as many as 6,000 visitors from all over the world stopped by her cabin for a bottle of her homemade root beer. After her death in 1986, Molter's homestead was dismantled and transported to Ely where volunteers painstakingly restored two of the cabins. Gift shop; video shown. Open daily Memorial Day–Labor Day (218-365-5161 or www.rootbeerlady.com). Wheelchair accessible. Fee charged.

Big Lake Wilderness Lodge

3012 Echo Tr, Ely, MN; 218-340-3533; www.biglakelodge.com

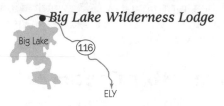

Located on a peninsula at an entry point for the BWCAW, Big Lake Wilderness Lodge is a great place to bring the kids. Not only do you get to stay in a roomy log cabin with a spectacular view of the lake that has prize walleye, but there's also a naturalist on hand to take the kids adventure hiking. They'll learn how to identify wildflowers and edible plants, and they'll see wildlife such as bear, moose, mink, otters and more. Some of the children's craft activities include making dream catchers, kites, salt candles, paper from pulp and sun catchers. Bring your mountain bike and ride the rugged trails or make use of the canoes, kayaks and paddleboats the lodge provides. Bird watchers delight in the wide variety of species. Store on premises carries grocery staples, bait and souvenirs. Lounge, sauna. Wheelchair accessible. $$–$$$$.

Minnesota Legends

Brainerd is approximately 150 miles north of the Twin Cities. Take Hwy 10 to Hwy 371 into Brainerd; www.brainerd.com; 800-450-2838 or 218-829-2838.

Paul Bunyan Nature Learning Center

7187 Wise Road, Brainerd, MN; 218-829-9620

The Paul Bunyan Nature Learning Center's pond hosts a pair of Trumpeter Swans and an active beaver lodge. Walk the 3-mile trail around the pond, then head off on the natural prairie trail. Interpretive center with a full-time naturalist on hand. Lots of educational projects, films and programs geared for kids. Free admission. Fee charged for programs. Closed Sundays.

Paul Bunyan Trail

Brainerd to Bemidji. www.paulbunyantrail.com or www.brainerd.com

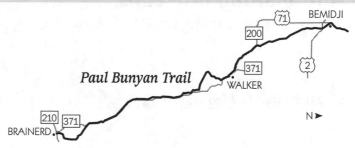

One of Minnesota's most famous and gigantic citizens is Paul Bunyan. Paul's footprints, along with those of his sidekick Babe, the Blue Ox, created the state's more than 10,000 lakes...or so the legend goes.

Hike, bike, in-line skate or snowmobile the 100-mile Paul Bunyan Trail (57 miles paved) from Brainerd to Bemidji. Very scenic with 14 towns, 21 lakes, 4 rivers and countless streams. For more information, contact the Brainerd Lakes Area Chamber of Commerce or log onto the Paul Bunyan Trail website, where you can play tic-tac-toe with Paul and Babe or read more about their legendary antics.

NOTE: Bike and ski rental available at Easy Riders Bicycle and Sportshop, 415 Washington St, Brainerd, MN; 218-829-5516. 3-hour bike rental: $15; 1-day rental: $23; 3-day rental: $45.

Charles A. Lindbergh House

1620 Lindbergh Dr S, Little Falls, MN (2 miles south of town); 320-616-5421; www.charleslindbergh.com (click on Boyhood Home)

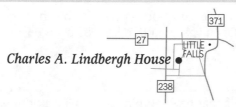

Charles A. Lindbergh Jr., the first person to fly across the Atlantic Ocean alone, spent his boyhood summers at this cottage on the Mississippi River.

The 1906 house contains original furnishings and family heirlooms. History center features a gift shop, family exhibits, as well as some of Lindbergh's inventions and aviation accomplishments. Open daily Memorial Day through Labor Day. Wheelchair accessible. Fee charged.

Minnesota Fishing Museum

Hwy 27 (west side of Little Falls); 320-616-5595

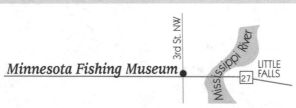

You can't take the kids on a "legends" trip without stopping in at the Minnesota Fishing Museum for a look at some fish legends. The museum's 2 showrooms house over 7,000 fishing artifacts, plus boat and motor displays, a 1920s fishing and hunting cabin and several state record fish replicas. The museum is wheelchair accessible and open year round. May–Sept, closed M; Oct–Apr, closed Su & M. Fee charged, but free for children ages 9 and under. Free admission on Tuesdays.

Pine Grove Zoo

Hwy 27 (west side of Little Falls); 320-616-5595; www.pinegrovezoo.com

Walk through the Pine Grove Zoo's deer pen. See bison, tigers and elk. Children's playground. Open year-round, daily. Fee charged.

Kids' Museums

Here are a few museums that have nothing to do with boring and everything to do with fun. Entertaining and educational, your kids won't be the only ones having a good time!

Science Museum of Minnesota

120 W Kellogg Blvd (across from the RiverCentre), St. Paul; 651-221-9444 or TTY: 651-221-4585; www.smm.org

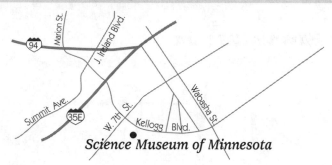

Science Museum of Minnesota

The Science Museum of Minnesota is home to a famous, long-dead resident—the mummy. Kids love mummies almost as much as they love dinosaurs. Luckily, the museum has both! Interactive displays allow you to control the choppers on a ferocious *T. Rex*, make tornadoes, wander the bloodstream superhighway or view your own cells. Climb aboard a real towboat, take in a 3D digital show or enjoy a movie in the Omnitheater. Head outdoors to the Big Back Yard for a challenging game of mini-golf. The 9-hole course is a twisting river of scientific questions about water patterns and erosion. Afterward, pan for gemstones in a giant sluice, hunt for fossils, take a walk through a prairie grass maze and enjoy the many other activities found in the Big Back Yard. Open daily. Closed on Mondays between mid-Sept.–mid Dec. Gift shop, two restaurants. Wheelchair accessible. Fee charged.

Minnesota Children's Museum

10 W 7th St (7th and Wabasha), St. Paul; 651-225-6001; www.mcm.org

Minnesota Children's Museum

One of the state's coolest places to explore, the Minnesota Children's Museum offers lots of imaginative and colorful hands-on activities.

Operate a crane or don an ant costume and crawl through an anthill maze. The only trouble is, this museum is so much fun that the adults want a turn at the exhibits, too! Open daily, Memorial Day–Labor Day. Closed Mondays after Labor Day. Wheelchair accessible. Fee charged.

Gibbs Farm Museum

2097 W Larpenter Ave, St. Paul; 651-646-8629; www.rchs.com/gbbsfm2.htm

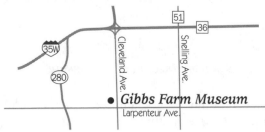

At the Gibbs Farm Museum, costumed interpreters demonstrate what life was like during the nineteenth century. Register the kids for a day at the schoolhouse. Open May–Oct, Tu–Su. Wheelchair accessible. Fee charged.

Things That Fly

Whether it's birds or a thrill ride, kids love things that fly. Try one of these to satisfy your children's (or your) dreams of flight.

Raptor Center

1920 Fitch Ave, St. Paul (on the University of Minnesota campus); 612-624-4745; www.theraptorcenter.org

See Great Horned Owls, Osprey, Red-tailed Hawks, eagles and many more birds of prey at the world-renowned Raptor Center. Learn interesting facts about the birds from on-staff naturalists. The center functions as a hospital for injured birds. Once recovered, birds are released back into the wild. Open year-round. Wheelchair accessible. Donation suggested for tour.

National Eagle Center

50 Pembroke Ave., Box 242, Wabasha; 877-332-4537 or 651-565-4989; www.nationaleaglecenter.org

Did you know that an eagle's average flight speed is 30 mph, with a dive speed around 100 mph? Did you know that an eagle's nest weighs hundreds of pounds? Learn all about these fascinating birds of prey at the beautiful and spacious (14,000 sq. ft.) National Eagle Center. Observation decks with spotting scopes are open 24/7. Trained guides are on-hand to answer your questions on weekends during the "eagle season" (Nov.-Mar). Visit Harriet, Angel, Columbia, and Donald—the Center's resident educational eagles, or see what an eagle sees by using special eagle vision in the interpretive area. The Center is open daily, year-round. Fee charged.

Valleyfair Amusement Park

One Valleyfair Dr, Shakopee; 800-FUN-RIDE or 952-445-6500; www.valleyfair.com

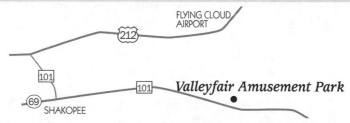

Now it's your turn to fly at Valleyfair! Ride the wet and wild Wave or summon your courage for a trip on the Power Tower! You'll blast 275' straight up, then drop the same distance in three seconds flat. It's sheer mind-numbing terror! Valleyfair has rides for every age (and stomach tolerance!) as well as live entertainment, a water park, concessions and the Pepsi IMAX theater. Open May–Sep. Wheelchair accessible. Fee charged.

Mall of America

Located at the junction of I-494 and Hwy 77 (Cedar Ave S.) in Bloomington; 952-883-8800; www.mallofamerica.com

Mall motto: There's a place for fun in your life—The Mall of America! Apparently, the more than 47 million people who visit the mall each year agree. The Mall of America is the largest of its kind in the U.S. and receives more visitors annually than Disney World, Graceland and the Grand Canyon combined. This "megamall" of malls provides plenty of shopping opportunities—more than 520 stores to mill through. With 50 restaurants for the choosing, you won't go hungry, either. The fourth floor offers a variety of entertainment including a comedy club, a 14-screen movie theater and seven nightclubs. Say your "I do's" in the Chapel of Love as thousands of couples have done, or go for a walk through the middle of Underwater Adventures' giant aquarium. Get nose to nose with sharks, stingrays and hundreds of other aquatic species as they swim on by.

At the mall's 3-story center, you'll find The Park at MOA. The indoor amusement park features over two dozen rides, including a full-scale roller coaster and an 18-hole miniature golf course. The LEGO Imagination. And don't forget to head on over to the Aveda Experience Spa for some well-deserved pampering.

Mall of America has free admission and parking. Wheelchair accessible. Fees charged for rides and attractions.

Lions, Tigers and Bears

Eagan is directly south of the Twin Cities off of I-35. Learn more about Eagan at www.ci.eagan.mn.us.

Minnesota Zoo

13000 Zoo Blvd, Apple Valley, MN; 800-366-7811 or 952-431-9500; www.mnzoo.com

Lions and tigers and bears, but—oh my—there's so much more! Like dolphins, primates, bats and camels. See thousands of animals in natural habitat settings. Take in the birds of prey show or a movie at the IMAX 3D Theatre. Hop the trolley for a ride to the Wells Fargo Family Farm to see a live, active farm, or tour the entire zoo from above on the extensive monorail system. Concessions; wheelchair accessible (electronic wheelchairs available). Fee charged at zoo entrance. Separate fee for the IMAX 3D Theatre. Parking fee.

Cascade Bay Water Park

1360 Civic Center Drive, Eagan, MN; 651-675-5577; www.cascadebay.com

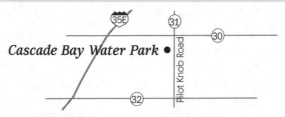

There's a saying in Minnesota: "It's not the heat, it's the humidity." If your family starts feeling the heat, take them to Cascade Bay Water Park. Shoot down Twin Falls or brave the Typhoon and Hurricane water slides. Feeling a bit more mellow? Then take a relaxing float on an inner tube in the Lazy River. The little ones have their own sprays, spouts and shipwreck slide. Open June through Aug. Concessions. Fee charged.

Grand Slam Sports

12425 River Ridge Blvd, Burnsville; 952-224-0413; www.grandslammn.com

Go to Grand Slam Sports. for a spirited game of laser tag or a challenging round of mini-golf. Watch your kids squeal with delight as they ram and dodge in bumper cars. Over 30,000 square feet boasts batting cages, video arcade, snack bar and more for the whole family. Open daily.

Camp in a Real Tepee!

Upper Sioux Agency State Park

State Hwy 67 (8 miles southeast of Granite Falls); 866-857-2757 (reservations); www.dnr.state.mn.us/state_parks/upper_sioux_agency/index.html

The only place you can tepee camp in Minnesota is the Upper Sioux Agency State Park. The Minnesota and Yellow Medicine Rivers provide spectacular fishing, hiking and birding. Spot Red-tailed Hawks, pelicans, Blue Herons and Belted Kingfishers. The park features a children's play area, horseshoe pits, volleyball courts and an equestrian camp. Only two tepees, so reserve early. Regular camping also offered. Fee charged.

Option: See **Minnesota's largest cottonwood**! Growing since 1860, the tree has a crown and trunk 30' in diameter. To get there, go 8 miles northwest of Montevideo on Hwy 59; turn left on Hwy 13 for 2.2 miles, then right 1 mile on Co 32. Right side of road; look for small sign.

Alexander Ramsey Park

Located on the northwest end of Redwood Falls, turn north on Lincoln St and follow signs. Redwood Falls Community Center: 507-644-2333
http://www.redwoodfalls.org/ramseypark

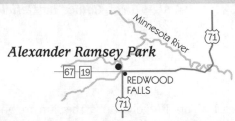

Redwood Falls is southeast of the Upper Sioux Agency on Hwy 71 and home to the state's largest municipal park, Alexander Ramsey Park, affectionately termed "The Little Yellowstone of Minnesota." It contains a zoo with bison, elk and peacocks, waterfalls, a DNR trout stream, paved hiking trails with very cool foot bridges, a ball diamond, a children's play area, picnic grounds and a campground. Admission fee charged.

Lower Sioux Agency

Interpretive center located 9 miles east of Redwood Falls on Co 2; 507-697-6321; www.mnhs.org/places/sites/lsa

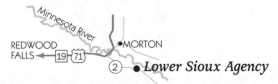

At the Lower Sioux Agency, learn the truth about the U.S.-Dakota Conflict of 1862. This Native American uprising left 500 settlers and an unknown number of Dakota dead. Open May–Labor Day. Call for winter hours. Wheelchair accessible. Fee charged.

NOTE: Outcrops of rock visible from the highway near the town of Morton—called **Morton Gneiss**—are 3.5 billion years old. These swirled multicolored rocks are gray, red and black and are quite possibly the oldest in the world!

Birch Coulee Battlefield

3 miles north of Morton at the junction of Co 2 & 18, 1 mile east of Hwy 71; 507-697-6321; www.mnhs.org/places/sites/bc

Soldiers from nearby Fort Ridgely, on a mission to bury dead civilians caught in the U.S.-Dakota conflict, found themselves surrounded by the Dakota and under siege for 36 hours before help arrived. Trail signs guide you through the entire battle. May–Oct, dawn until dusk. Free.

Fort Ridgely

7 miles south of Fairfax on Hwy 4; 507-426-7888 or 507-697-6321; www.mnhs.org/places/sites/fr

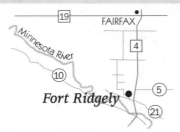

Built in 1853, Fort Ridgely was intended as a police state for keeping the peace between new settlers and the Dakota. Learn about the daily lives of the people who lived and worked in this Civil War-era military fort. Try on prairie clothing, soldiers' wool uniforms and handle a musket. Lots of hands-on exhibits. Open Memorial weekend–Labor Day, F–Su. Minnesota State Park permit required.

Cannon River Tubing

Welch Mill Canoeing and Tubing

Located in Welch on Co 7 off of Hwy 61; 651-388-9857 and 800-657-6760; www.welchmillcanoeandtube.com

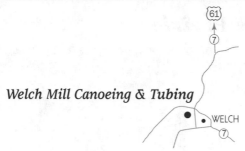

Welch Mill Canoeing & Tubing

Welch is a scene right out of a movie—literally. A big Hollywood production company filmed the motion picture *Here On Earth* in this picturesque village, using many of the locals as walk-ons. So look around, have an ice cream cone, then take a lazy ride down the Cannon River by canoe or inner tube. Ross Nelson of Welch Mill Canoeing and Tubing will happily provide you with a rental. If he's not too busy, he'll probably even shoot a few hoops with you. Rental price includes life jackets, paddles and shuttle service. If your bus driver happens to be an Irish storyteller named Bill, tell him his sister says hi! Open daily Memorial Day weekend–Labor Day weekend. Call for off-season hours. 5- or 12-mile trip.

Option: A restful haven for weary bikers, Welch is the midway point on the 20-mile **Cannon Valley Trail**.

Just Like Laura Ingalls Wilder

These attractions visit the home territory of beloved author Laura Ingalls Wilder. It's also your chance to be a real pioneer family. Show your youngsters what it was like to live on the prairie without electricity or indoor plumbing.

Sod House on the Prairie

12598 Magnolia Ave, Sanborn, MN; 507-723-5138; www.sodhouse.org. Virginia McCone, Innkeeper.

Could there be anything more fun than an overnight stay in a sod house? To reach the authentic 1880 sod house replica, just follow a trail through 8' tall prairie grass. The house has 2' thick walls and a grass roof. Inside, you'll find whitewashed walls, oil lamps for light, two double beds, a fainting couch, a wood-burning stove, a wash pitcher and bowl, prairie clothes to dress up in and—oh yes—a backyard outhouse! Explore the trapper's cabin complete with furs, traps and Indian artifacts. Full breakfast delivered to your door in a basket. Bed & Breakfast operates June–Sept. $$–$$$. Tours of sod house run Apr–Oct. Fee charged.

Walnut Grove

800-528-7280; www.walnutgrove.org

In 1874, seven-year-old Laura Ingalls Wilder and her family traveled from Wisconsin's Big Woods to Walnut Grove, Minnesota, settling on the banks of Plum Creek. The community preserves Laura's past and celebrates with an annual festival in her honor. Visit the Laura Ingalls Wilder Museum located at 330 8th St. Here you'll see "Grandma's House" among the four buildings at the main museum site. The Ingalls' homestead site is 1½ miles north of the museum. Apr–Oct, open daily. Fee charged

Jeffers Petroglyphs

27160 County Road 2, Comfrey, MN; 507-628-5591;www.mnhs.org/places/sites/jp; Located 3 miles east of Hwy 71 on Co 10; then 1 mile south on Co 2.

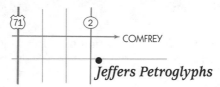

The glacier-scarred bedrock contains thousands of ancient rock carvings known as petroglyphs. This is a sacred place, one that has been used by American Indian tribes for more than 5,000 years. Search the rock outcrops for carvings of bison, turtles, thunderbirds and human figures. The surrounding native prairie boasts cacti and other rare plants.

Visitor center with interactive activities, exhibits and video. Open Memorial Day–Labor Day, M & W–Su; May & Sep, F–Su. Wheelchair accessible. Fee charged.

NOTE: The Petroglyphs are easier to see during the morning, late afternoon or on a cloudy day.

Options: Although it's a bit out of the way, a trip to **Blue Mounds State Park** is well worth the added miles. The park takes its name from the cliff of Sioux quartzite that appeared blue to the settlers as they journeyed west. On the park's southern end is an unexplained 1,250' line of rocks that aligns with the sun on the first day of spring and fall. The northern end attracts visitors to a viewing platform for a look at a bison herd. Also has a campground, swimming beach, wildflower prairie with cacti and 7' tall grasses. Quartzite interpretive center. Park located in the southwest corner of Minnesota, 3 miles north of Luverne off Hwy 75; 507-283-1307.

Farming

Farmamerica

Located 80 miles south of the Twin Cities. Take I-35 south to Hwy 14. Farmamerica is 4 miles west of Waseca on Co 2; watch for signs; 507-835-2052; www.farmamerica.org

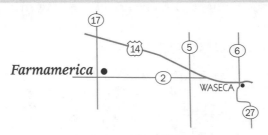

What kid doesn't want to grow up on a farm, and who can blame them? There are so many exciting things to see and do, from tending the animals to making forts out of hay. Unfortunately, the number of Minnesota family farms is dwindling, but you can still get a hands-on farming experience by visiting Farmamerica—the state's agricultural interpretive center. A self-guided walking tour takes you through 150 years of farming, including an 1850s settlement and a 1920s dairy setup.

Farmamerica hosts four annual festivals. Demonstrations include sheep shearing, shingle making, hay baling, corn-shucking, meat smoking and weaving on a century-old loom. There are also draft horses, antique tractors, threshing, quilt show and many more farm activities. Gift shop and silo lookout, slide show and displays. Open Memorial Day–Labor Day. Wheelchair accessible. Fee charged.

Options: Cabela's is the largest hunting, fishing and outdoor retail center in the Midwest and only 20 miles east of Farmamerica on I-35 in Owatonna (take exit 45). The store features a 35' tall mountain with mounted animals in realistic settings, 54,000 gallons of fresh-water aquariums, interactive demonstration areas and a restaurant that serves elk sandwiches. Famous shoppers to Cabela's include Garth Brooks, Trisha Yearwood and Walter Payton. Open daily; 507-451-4545; www.cabelas.com. Wheelchair accessible. • The **Village of Yesteryear** is at 1448 Austin Road, next to the Owatonna fairgrounds. A unique boardwalk meanders through the 15-building village, providing a look at life during the turn of the nineteenth century. May–Sept. Closed Monday. 507-451-1420; www.steelecohistoricalsociety.org/village.php. Fee charged.

Nature Experience

Eagle Bluff Environmental Learning Center

Take Hwy 52 south through Rochester until Fountain; follow Co Rd 8 toward Lanesboro; follow signs. 888-800-9558; www.eagle-bluff.org

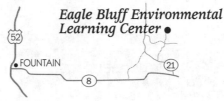

If you got lost in a woods, would you know how to survive and which plants are edible? About once a month Eagle Bluff offers family getaway weekends that are fun and teach important outdoor skills. Naturalist-guided trips range from snowshoeing to maple syruping, depending on the season. The Discovery Center features an indoor climbing wall, a live raptor center and an auditorium.

Weekends include a full buffet dinner, evening entertainment, overnight lodging (dormitory style), breakfast and two programs—$$.

Options: Less than 10 miles from Eagle Bluff, you'll find **Avian Acres Wild Bird Supply.** Located 1½ miles southwest of Lanesboro off County Road 8; follow the signs; 800-967-BIRDS (2473); Avian Acres specializes in wild bird supplies and attracting backyard birds. Relax in their rural setting while enjoying tame deer and the antics of colorful songbirds. Open Tu–Sa and select Su & M. www.aawildbirdsupply.com • The **State DNR Fish Hatchery**, located a few miles south of Lanesboro, produces more trout per year than any other state hatchery. Free tours. • **Van Gundy's Elk Farm** is 3 miles north of Houston on Hwy 76 (less than 30 miles from Eagle Bluff). Herd has over 50 elk. Learn what elk eat, what their mannerisms are, how to care for them and see the spring calves. Call ahead: 507-896-2380.

St. Cloud Gardens

Clemens Rose Gardens ● ST. CLOUD
Munsinger Gardens

Eloise Butler Wildflower Garden
Mpls. Sculpture Garden
Noerenberg Gardens
Minnesota Landscape Arboretum

Metro Area Gardens

Como Park
Conservatory
Lyndale Rose Garden

Scherer Flower Garden
and Caponi Art Park

Serene Feast

Southern Minnesota Gardens

REDWOOD FALLS
MORGAN
Gilfillan Estate

LE SEUER
NEW ULM
ST. PETER

Mayo Park & Arboretum

August Schell
Brewery

Linnaeus Arboretum & Sculpture Garden

THEME: GARDEN TOURS

St. Cloud Gardens

Metro Area Gardens

A Serene Feast for the Soul

Southern Minnesota Gardens

Garden
Tours
NEXT RIGHT

*M*ore people than ever before list gar-
dening as their #1 hobby. This chapter
showcases some of the most spectacular gardens nurtured in Minnesota. So
even if you don't care to keep a garden
yourself, you can still enjoy the fruits of
someone else's labors.

St. Cloud Gardens

Clemens Rose Gardens

Killian Blvd and 14th St, St. Cloud, MN; 320-255-7238;
www.munsingerclemens.com

Parallel to the Munsinger Gardens, Bill Clemens donated the beautiful Clemens Rose Gardens to the city of St. Cloud as a dedication to his wife, Virginia. Suffering from multiple sclerosis, Mrs. Clemens need only look out her window to gaze at the more than 1,200 rosebushes directly across the street. Considered to be one of the largest public rose gardens in the state, the Clemens Rose Gardens consist of six connecting formal gardens. Open daily: Sunrise–sunset. Free.

Munsinger Gardens

Riverside Dr S and Michigan Ave, St. Cloud, MN; 320-255-7238;
www.munsingerclemens.com

Located on the scenic banks of the Mississippi River, the Munsinger Gardens came to life in 1915 as part of a park. The gardens now boast huge shade trees, a lily pond with fountain, a gazebo, benches to rest upon and a pair of peacocks. Open daily: Sunrise–sunset. Free.

Option: The **Stearns History Museum** is a great place to learn about Central Minnesota's history. Two floors of spectacular exhibits include a life-size replica of a granite quarry, the controversial 1919 Pan Automobile, and a century-old dairy setup. The large Research Center specializes in genealogical information from Luxembourg and Germany. It also houses tons of intriguing information about the granite and dairy industries, sports, and architecture. Kids have a blast in the Children's Gallery. They can shop in a kid-sized grocery store, visit with a talking globe, be the ring master of a circus, build a log barn and more. The Stearns History Museum has a gift store, movies, gardens, and hiking trails. They are at 235 South 33rd Ave, St. Cloud; 866-253-8424 or 320-253-8424; www.stearns-museum.org. Open daily, year round. Fee charged; children age 4 and under are free.

Metro Area Gardens

Como Park Conservatory

Located between Hamline and Lexington Aves on Midway Blvd in St. Paul; 651-487-8200; www.comozooconservatory.org

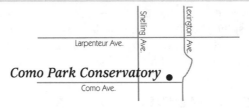

With just one foot inside the glass-enclosed Como Park Conservatory, you'll swear you're deep inside a jungle paradise surrounded by calling birds and flowing water. The humidity hangs thick on even the most frigid of Minnesota days, and color abounds from exotic orange-blue birds of paradise and sassy hot pink orchids. Banana trees, hanging vines, wispy ferns, tropical fish, a sunken garden and so much more. The only thing missing is Tarzan! Open daily. Wheelchair accessible. Fee charged.

NOTE: The adjoining Como Park Zoo is free and open daily.

Minneapolis Sculpture Garden

Located on Vineland Pl across from the Guthrie Theater and the Walker Art Center, Minneapolis; 612-375-7600; http://garden.walkerart.org

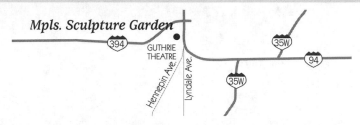

One of the most photographed Twin Cities' landmarks is the Spoonbridge and Cherry sculpture found in the Minneapolis Sculpture Garden. Hedges divide 10 acres of space into "rooms" that contain more than 40 interesting works of art, making this garden the largest of its kind in the country. The conservatory encloses a gigantic glass fish surrounded by palm trees and hibiscus. Open daily. Free.

Option: The **Walker Art Center** is one of the country's leading contemporary art museums and houses a permanent collection of 20th-century paintings, photographs and sculptures. The newly designed facility features galleries filled with modern and contemporary art, two Wolfgang Puck restaurants, films, performances and outdoor terraces with spectacular views. Closed Mondays. Wheelchair accessible. Fee charged, but free for children under age 12.

Eloise Butler Wildflower Garden & Bird Sanctuary

Located off Wirth Pkwy, south of Hwy 55; 612-370-4903; www.minneapolisparks.org

The Eloise Butler Wildflower Garden is thought to be the oldest public wildflower garden in the U.S. Founded in 1907, botanist Eloise Butler understood the importance of conservation long before it became a cool thing to do. Hike the garden's 14 acres of trails through shady woodlands, bogs and prairies. Interpretive center open daily, Apr–Oct. Free. Guided tours and special programs offered weekends—fee may be charged.

Lyndale Rose Garden

4125 E Lake Harriet Pkwy, Minneapolis; 612-230-6400; www.minneapolisparks.org

Also established in 1907, the Lyndale Rose Garden is the second oldest public rose garden in the country. Expansive rose gardens, exotic and native trees, perennials and fountains. Open daily.

Option: Bring your binoculars because next to the gardens are 13 acres of wetlands and woods known as the **Thomas Sadler Roberts Bird Sanctuary**.

Noerenberg Memorial Gardens

2840 North Shore Dr, Orono; 763-559-9000; www.threeriversparkdistrict.org

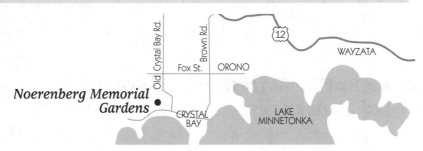

Located near Lake Minnetonka's Crystal Bay in Orono, the Noerenberg Gardens feature an amazing collection of daylilies and azaleas, as well as a vast and vibrant rainbow of annuals and perennials. Open daily, May 1 through mid-Oct. Free.

A Serene Feast for the Soul

This batch of gardens begins in Eagan directly south of the Twin Cities off of I-35, then ends up in the Minnesota Landscape Arboretum in Chanhassen.

Scherer Flower Garden

1535 Cliff Rd, Eagan, MN; 651-454-4521; www.scherergardens.com

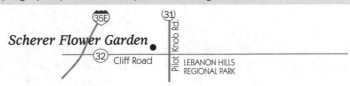

The Scherer Flower Garden was one man's vision, and now is a magic place for all. Enter into acres of lovely gardens and feast your eyes on this picture-perfect setting with its walkways and fountains. Your senses awaken to lush textures, buzzing insects and exotic fragrances. You'll feel as if you've found the Garden of Eden and you won't ever want to leave. Open daily. Donations accepted.

Caponi Art Park

1205 Diffley Rd, Eagan, MN; 651-454-9412; www.caponiartpark.org

Put your Chi in harmony by exploring Caponi Art Park. This is an outdoor sculpture garden designed within an oak landscape. Arranged tours available the end of May–Oct, Tu–Su. Free

Minnesota Landscape Arboretum

3675 Arboretum Dr (9 miles west of I-494 on Hwy 5), Chanhassen, MN; 952-443-1400; www.arboretum.umn.edu. From Diffley Rd in Eagan, take Hwy 77 north to I-494 and head west.

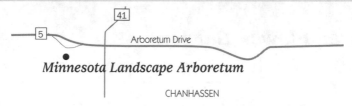

The Minnesota Landscape Arboretum showcases over 900 acres of unique gardens developed specifically for the harsh northern climate. You'll find there's not a bad time of year to visit the Arboretum. It's as beautiful during a January deep freeze as it is in the height of the growing season.

The Arboretum features a Japanese garden, a hosta glade, herb and wildflower gardens and dazzling annual and perennial beds. The rose garden contains 150 hybrid varieties, surrounded by a trellised collection of clematis, fountains and a gazebo.

Walk through acres of outdoor "rooms" that display shrubs, hedges and conifers. There are fruit tree orchards, deciduous trees, and lots of cozy alcoves with benches. Take a free 90-minute guided walking tour or a 1-hour tram ride (fee charged). Explore the greenhouse or research a new discovery at the Andersen Horticultural Library. The Meyer-Deats Conservatory houses exotic and tropical indoor plants and succulents.

Bring your own lunch and have a picnic at the Margot Picnic Shelter or enjoy homemade soups, salads and sandwiches in the cafeteria. Open daily. Gift shop. Wheelchair accessible. Fee charged for those ages 15 and older; free admission every Thurs after 4:30 p.m. and throughout the winter months (Nov–Feb).

NOTE: Serene and picturesque even during the winter months, the Arboretum offers cross country skiers miles of groomed trails. View burgundy dogwood paired with cedar greens and angular stands of birch trees against a silver-gray sky. Chase away those winter doldrums by attending a traditional English Tea. The tea includes all the trimmings—starched table linens, fine china, scrumptious finger sandwiches, scones and petit fours. Reserve a table by the fireplace and enjoy! Call the Arboretum for reservations and details. W afternoons—$$.

Southern Minnesota Gardens

Le Sueur, known as "the city of flowers," is 55 miles southwest of the Twin Cities off Hwy 169. Take the Hwy 112 exit into town. www.cityofleseuer.com

Mayo Park & Arboretum

LeSueur. On the north end of town on Co 28.

• *Mayo Park & Arboretum*

⑧

(169)

LE SUEUR

• Mayo House

Some years ago, the mother and daughter team behind the greeting card company *it takes two®* decided to build their corporate headquarters in Le Sueur for one simple reason: the flower gardens. The Mayo Park and Arboretum features rose beds, a white garden, herbs, over 20 hosta varieties, bulbs and perennials. Free.

> **Option:** While you're in town, tour the **W.W. Mayo House** (118 N Main St. 507-665-3250. www.mayohouse.org). Costumed interpreters guide you through the 1859 home of Mayo Clinic founder W. W. Mayo. The doctor set up his first medical practice in a room upstairs. After the good doctor left for Rochester, the Cosgroves—founders of the Green Giant Company—moved into the house in 1874. Open mid-May–mid-Oct. Fee charged. Free for children age 5 and under.

Linnaeus Arboretum & Sculpture Garden

St. Peter, on the grounds of Gustavus Adolphus College. Main entrance is on College Ave.; 507-933-7003; www.gustavus.edu/arboretum

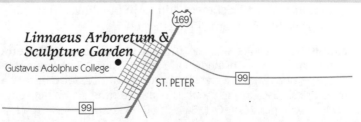

(169)

*Linnaeus Arboretum &
Sculpture Garden*

Gustavus Adolphus College •

ST. PETER

99

99

The Linnaeus Arboretum has areas representing the three major natural ecosystems found in Minnesota: conifer forests, deciduous forests and prairies. A fourth area, cultivated gardens and trees from other regions, sur-

79

rounds the Melva Lind Interpretive Center. Lilac walk, bluebird trail, 1866 Swedish pioneer cabin, exhibits and programs. Free.

August Schell Brewery

New Ulm. Go south on Broadway, then turn west on 18th St; follow signs; 800-770-5020 or 507-354-5528; www.schellsbrewery.com

August Schell Brewery •

A brewery in the gardens chapter? No, this is not a joke. Schell's is the second-oldest, family-owned brewery in the nation and they do offer a tour of the operation for a small fee, but the gorgeous gardens with peacocks strutting about are open to the public for free. Arbors, roses, annual and perennial beds. Also a deer park, museum and gift shop.

Gilfillan Estate

Located on Hwy 67 between Redwood Falls and Morgan; 507-249-2210

The Gilfillan Estate is a restored 1882 farm with a beautiful yard and flower gardens. The estate includes the home's original furniture, a summer kitchen, antique farm machinery and farm buildings. Guided tours. Open Jun–Labor Day, Sa & Su. Small fee charged.

Option: Since you're so close, the **Redwood County Museum** is worth a visit. Located west of Redwood Falls on Hwy 19, the museum occupies what was once a Poor Farm. Thirty rooms display local history and period furnishings. Also on the grounds is an old-time schoolhouse and antique machinery. Open May–Oct, Sa–Su; 507-641-2828.

Como Park Conservatory (pg. 74)

August Schell Brewery Gardens (pg. 80)

Mesabi Iron Range

Soudan

Virginia · Biwabik

Mountain Iron

Chisolm · Hoyt Lakes

Hibbing · Eveleth

Grand Rapids · Calumet

[1]

[61]

[53] [135]

[2]

[169]

[35]

DULUTH

Twin Cities Caves

Western Wisconsin's Pierce Co.

Wabasha Street Caves

Battle Creek Park

Crystal Cave and Eau Galle Dam

Berg's Rock Shop

Nugget Lake County Park

[35]

[52]

[61]

ROCHESTER

Southeastern Minnesota's Bluff Country

Mystery Cave

Niagara Cave

THEME: *GEOLOGY & CAVE TOURS*

The Mesabi Iron Range

Twin Cities Caves

GEOLOGY/

CAVE TOURS

Western Wisconsin's Pierce County

Southeastern Minnesota's Bluff Country

Ironworld Discovery Center, Chisholm (pg. 89)

Mineview in the Sky, Virginia (pg. 91)

Is there anything more exciting than exploring a cave? It's cold, it's wet, it's dark and it's a place where our imaginations are free to run wild! In a cave, we, too, can be Ali Baba hunting for treasures or the heroic Batman fighting off thugs.

This chapter explores some very interesting Minnesota caves; one has a waterfall and another boasts a beautiful lake. There's even a cave with a fireplace!

The Mesabi Iron Range

From the Twin Cities, take Hwy 169 approximately 175 miles north to Grand Rapids. Iron Trail Convention & Visitors Bureau; 800-777-8497; www.irontrail.org.

The official Mesabi Iron Range consists of Hibbing and those towns east to Hoyt Lakes. However, this section covers more than the Iron Range and includes an area 100 miles north from Grand Rapids to Soudan. No caves on this venture, but lots of fascinating mining operations and geology stuff.

Note: The Aurora Borealis (Northern Lights) occur regularly in this region, creating a rainbow of colors and shapes against the night sky. They are especially active during the spring and fall.

Taconite State Trail: Grand Rapids

Grand Rapids Chamber of Commerce, 800-472-6366; www.grandmn.com or www.dnr.state.mn.us/state_trails/taconite/index.html

Taconite State Trail

The 165-mile **Taconite State Trail** (paved for the first 6 miles outside of Grand Rapids) provides a great view of old mining operations. It's perfect for bikers, hikers, horseback riders and snowmobilers.

Options: Grand Rapids is the birthplace of singer/actress Judy Garland. Skip along the yellow brick sidewalk downtown before touring the plain, two-story white house (has some original furniture) that was Judy's childhood home. Also visit the **Judy Garland Children's Museum** located at 2727 Hwy 169 S. The museum houses props from the movie *The Wizard of Oz*. Open daily Memorial Day - Labor Day ; 800-664-5839; www.judygarlandmuseum.com. Fee charged. • A visit to the **Forest History Center** (2609 Co 76) is a trip back into the early 1900s. Learn what life was like for loggers through costumed interpreters. Also an interpretive center with movies and exhibits. Open daily. Fee charged. www.mnhs.org/places/sites/fhc • Learn how wood becomes paper at the **Blandin Paper Mill**, 115 1st St SW (alongside the Mississippi River). Forty-five minute tour for ages 12 and up. Open Jun–Aug, W–F, For more info call 218-327-6282. Free.

Hill Annex Mine State Park: Calumet

Calumet is roughly 14 miles northeast of Grand Rapids on Hwy 169. Hill Annex
Mine State Park is north of Calumet on Hwy 169; 218-247-7215

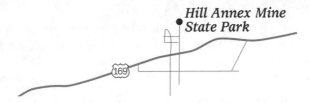

*Hill Annex Mine
State Park*

169

The **Hill Annex Mine State Park** was a thriving, open pit iron ore mine
until its closure in 1978. Take the 90-minute bus tour 500' down into the
heart of the pit. Tour winds past huge mining machinery and company
buildings. Special fossil hunting tours available. Tours run Wed–Su
Memorial Day-Labor Day, Boat tours are also available.

Mine clubhouse with interpretive exhibits and Calumet Depot/gift shop.
Open Memorial Day–Labor Day, closed Su. Fee charged.

Hull Rust Mahoning Mine: Hibbing

From Hibbing, continue another 15 miles northeast on Hwy 169. Hibbing
Chamber of Commerce: 218-262-3895; www.hibbing.org or www.irontrail.org;
Hull Rust Mine/Mine View: 218-262-4900 or 218-262-4166 (tourist center)

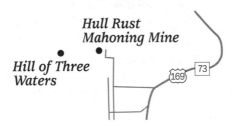

*Hull Rust
Mahoning Mine*

*Hill of Three
Waters*

169 73

Called the "Grand Canyon of the North," Hibbing's **Hull Rust Mahoning
Mine** is a National Historic Landmark and the largest open pit mine in the
world. Still active, the 3-mile long, 600' deep pit consists of more than 50
mines. Unbelievable panoramic view from observation deck located on the
north side of town; follow 3rd Ave E. Walking trail, BMX track, RC flying field
and information center. Open mid-May through Sept. Call for hours. Free.

NOTE: Known as the **Hill of Three Waters** or the **Triple Divide**, this
point of land is the only one of its kind in the U.S. A raindrop falling to
earth at precisely this spot could divide three ways and eventually flow to

the Atlantic Ocean, the Gulf of Mexico and Hudson Bay. Although it is not publicly accessible due to mining industry operations, the Triple Divide is 2 miles northwest of town.

Options: For a truly eerie sight, tour what's left of **North Hibbing** (follow E 3rd Ave north from downtown Hibbing about 2 miles). The original town relocated in 1918 to make room for the expanding Hull Rust mine. Log haulers towed houses and steam shovels scooped up graves, leaving behind sidewalks, street lamps and signs. Concrete steps on empty lots lead nowhere. • Andrew Anderson and Carl Wickman saw opportunity in the Hibbing move and capitalized on it. The entrepreneurs shuttled people from the old town to the new in their Hupmobile. By charging 15 cents a ride, their business eventually grew into Greyhound Bus Lines. Five historical buses and the Hupmobile are on display at the **Greyhound Bus Museum**, located on 3rd Ave E. Open daily, mid-May through Sept. 218-263-5814. www.greyhoundbusmuseum.org. Wheelchair accessible. Fee charged. • Visit the **Hibbing Historical Society Museum** (Memorial Building at 5th Ave and 23rd St) for an accurate documentation of the town's relocation. Closed Sundays. 218-263-8522. Small fee charged. • **Paulucci Space Theatre**—Sensational wrap-around theatre. Hibbing Community College, 1502 E 23rd St. Daily shows. 218-262-6720. Fee charged. • Robert Zimmerman (better known as Bob Dylan) grew up in Hibbing. The **Hibbing Public Library** features an exhibit of the legendary singer/songwriter. Open M–Sa. (Closed on Saturdays during the summer.) 218-262-5959 or www.hibbing.mn.us. Free.

Ironworld Discovery Center: Chisholm

801 SW Hwy 169, Suite 1; Ironworld Discovery Center is west of Chisholm on Hwy 169; 218-254-7959 or 800-372-6437; www.ironworld.com

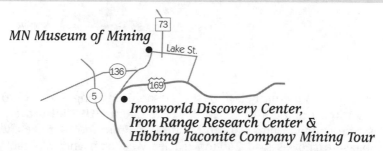

MN Museum of Mining

Ironworld Discovery Center, Iron Range Research Center & Hibbing Taconite Company Mining Tour

Perched atop the Glen iron mine, **Ironworld Discovery Center** is a giant among interpretive centers. Plan to spend an entire day here as it has something for everyone—costumed interpreters, mining equipment for climbing on, Native American camps, trapper's cabins, ethnic foods, a children's amusement park and a mine-educational 19-hole mini-golf course.

Hop the Mesabi Railway Trolley for a 2.5 mile ride along the Glen mine. The trolley stops at the 1915 Glen Depot for a living history lesson of what life was like for the residents who lived there at the turn of the century. Open year-round, call for days and times. Wheelchair accessible. Fee charged.

Located within Ironworld is the **Iron Range Research Library and Archives**. The library contains one of the largest collections of genealogical and local history research materials in the Upper Midwest. Open year-round; 218-254-7959; www.ironrangeresearchcenter.org.

Options: If you're interested in learning how a real mine operates, take the 90-minute **Hibbing Taconite Company Mine Tour**. Tours offered mid-Jun through mid-Aug, selected W & Th at noon. Wear slacks and comfortable shoes. Must be at least 10 years of age. Call Ironworld Discovery Center for details. 218-254-7959. Fee charged. • **The Minnesota Museum of Mining** is located in Memorial Park at the top of Main Street. This is a hands-on museum with exhibits indoors and out, as well as a replica of an underground mine and model steam train. Climb aboard a 125-ton dump truck. Also see a 1910 Atlantic steam shovel and a 1907 locomotive. Open Memorial Day–Labor Day, Mon-Sa 9-5, Sun 1-5. 218-254-5543; www.fnbchisholm.com/mining Fee charged.

USS/Minntac: Mountain Iron

Mountain Iron is less than 15 miles east of Chisholm on Hwy 169; watch for signs.

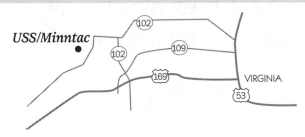

Mountain Iron is the birthplace of the Mesabi Iron Range—the 1890 discovery of iron ore there launched the era to come. **USS/Minntac** is the largest operating taconite plant in Minnesota. From the overlooks, watch 37-cubic-yard shovels load 240-ton trucks. Wacootah and Minntac Mine Overlooks are located at the north end of Mountain Avenue.

Mineview in the Sky: Virginia

Located on Hwy 53; www.virginia-mn.com

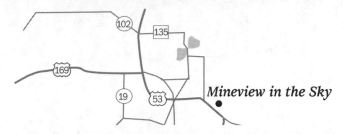

Mineview in the Sky is a 20-story overlook of the area's deepest open pit mine. And if that doesn't make you feel small, have your picture taken next to the 240-ton mining truck parked next to the visitor center. 218-741-2344 or 218-741-2717. Free.

> **Option:** See the **World's Largest Floating Loon** on Silver Lake in Virginia. At 20' long and 10' high, you won't have any trouble spotting it.

Leonidas Overlook: Eveleth

Drive south from Virginia for 5 miles on Hwy 53; 218-741-7444 or www.ironrange.us/towns/eveleth.htm

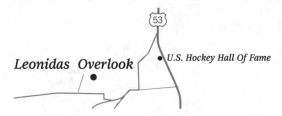

Leonidas Overlook is the highest man-made point on the Iron Trail and provides a panoramic view of the EvTac and Minntac mining operations.

> **Options:** Need a little break from all the mine touring? Then visit the **United States Hockey Hall of Fame** in Eveleth. Inspect jerseys and memorabilia from over 100 hockey greats. Watch recorded scenes from the 1980 "miracle on ice" U.S. Olympic Hockey game. Located along Hwy 53 on Hat Trick Avenue. 218-744-5167 or 800-443-7825. www.ushockeyhall.com. Gift shop. Wheelchair accessible. Fee charged. • Eveleth also boasts the **World's Largest Hockey Stick**. It measures 110' with a weight over five tons! Downtown district.

Iron Trail: Biwabik

From Eveleth, retrace route north on Hwy 53 toward Virginia; take Hwy 135 north-east; 218-865-4183; www.cityofbiwabik.com

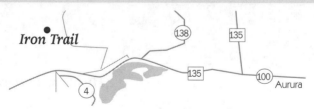

Still part of the **Iron Trail**, Biwabik is best known for its phenomenal all-season outdoor recreation. With over 2,000 miles of scenic groomed trails and an average snowfall of 100 inches, countless snowmobile magazines proclaim the area a snowmobiler's paradise.

> **Option: Eli Wirtanen Finnish Farmstead**. Homesteaded in 1904, the self-guided tour consists of 16 buildings including the main house, horse barn, shingle mill and hay shed, along with historical equipment. Half-hour drive south of Biwabik on Hwy 4. Watch for signs (farm on the right side of road). 218-638-2859. www.wirtanenfrm.org. Free.

Longyear Drill Site: Hoyt Lakes

Hoyt Lakes; from Biwabik, continue east on Hwy 135; turn on Hwy 110 (13 miles total); 218-749-3150; www.ironrange.org/attractions/mining/longyear-drill

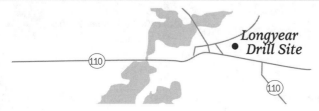

Edmund Longyear introduced diamond drilling to the area in 1890. A ¼-mile wilderness path leads to the **Longyear Drill Site**. See the actual steam engine used to drive the drill thousands of feet below the surface. Open year-round. No admission fee.

Soudan Underground Mine State Park: Soudan

Retrace route to Hwy 135. Follow Hwy 135 north; go east on Hwy 169.
www.dnr.state.mn.us/state_parks/soudan_underground_mine/index.html

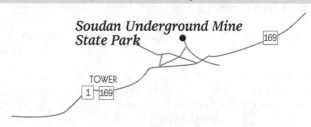

The **Soudan Underground Mine State Park** is home to Minnesota's oldest and deepest (27 levels) underground iron mining sites. The 90-minute tour includes an elevator ride that drops ½ mile underground, using two spiral staircases and an electric train ride as fun as anything you'll find at Disneyland. A self-guided surface tour includes a drill shop, an engine house, a crusher and a dry house. Visitor center offers informative movie on mining history. Park is off of Hwy 169, with plenty of signs pointing the way. Memorial Day–Sep, open daily; 218-753-2245. Fee charged, free for children under 5.

NOTE: Wear warm clothing. The wind and 50-degree temperature in the mine shaft make for a chilly train ride.

Twin Cities Caves

Wabasha Street Caves

215 Wabasha St S (on the right after the bridge), St. Paul; 651-224-1191;
www.wabashastreetcaves.com

St. Paul has a dark past. In the 1930s, notorious gangsters like Ma Barker, Babyface Nelson and John Dillinger terrorized local businesses and citizens. A popular thug hideout was the Wabasha Street Caves. History comes alive with one look at the fireplace marred by bullet holes. Tours year-round, Th 5pm, Sa & Su 11a.m.; Also offered is a 2-hour tour of gangster-associated sites on Sa. Fee charged.

NOTE: For more tours with a gangster slant, call **Gangster Tours**: 952-292-1220.

Option: While you're in the area, take a cruise on a paddleboat operated by Padelford Packet Boat Co. Daily cruises from Harriet Island on the Mississippi River. May–Sept. Fee charged, free for children age 4 and under. Other trips offered include lunch and dinner cruises, Sunday brunches and fall colors cruises. But that's not all. You can also take in a real theatrical show on a paddleboat. Shows scheduled year round Tues–Sat; matinees and evenings. Call the **Mississippi River Rides** for more information on cruises and shows: 800-543-3908 or 651-227-1100; www.showboattheater.com

Battle Creek Park

2300 Upper Afton Rd, Maplewood, 651-748-2500;
www.co.ramsey.mn.us/parks/parks/countyparks.htm

Take a picnic basket and plenty of energy because you'll want to explore every inch of this park. Lots of good hiking trails and caves, caves, caves!

Western Wisconsin's Pierce County

Pierce County is home to the largest earthen dam in the Midwest and the longest natural cave in Wisconsin. Pack a picnic basket and pan for gold at Nugget Lake!

Berg's Rock Shop

1231 Pearl St N, Prescott; 715-262-5841; www.bergsrockshop.com. From bridge, travel east on Hwy 10 for 1 mile; turn left on Pearl St and watch for "Rock Shop" sign on left.

The informative folks at Berg's Rock Shop have been in business for more than 30 years. They have more than 100 varieties of rocks and mineral specimens, as well as lapidary supplies and stone gifts and jewelry. Of special interest are Lake Superior agates. Open daily.

Nugget Lake County Park

N4351 Co Rd HH, Plum City, 715-639-5611; www.co.pierce.wi.us/nugget_lake/nl_main.htm. Located 31 miles from Prescott. Travel east on Hwy 10 through Ellsworth toward Plum City. Watch for signs.

From 1887 to 1906, the Land Flour Gold Mining Company operated a placer mine (mechanical way to pan for gold) on Plum Creek, now the north end of the 750-acre Nugget Lake County Park. Open year-round 6 a.m.-10 p.m., the picturesque park offers camping, fishing, picnicking, boating, canoeing, hiking, nature programs and an outdoor amphitheater.

Licenses, bait, ice, canoe and boat rentals available at the park office. If you plan to do some prospecting, remember to bring your own pan. Entrance fee, senior citizens free.

Crystal Cave

W965 State Rd 29, Spring Valley; 800-236-2283; www.acoolcave.com

Open to the public since 1942, Crystal Cave is Wisconsin's longest cave. Tour multiple levels filled with stalactites, stalagmites, dripstone, curtains and helectites. If your prospecting luck at Nugget Lake was less than successful, buy a bag of gem stock and pan it in the sluice trough. Hour-long guided tours offered Memorial Day through Labor Day, daily: 9–6. Call for off-season hours. Gift shop with all kinds of bat paraphernalia, rocks and homemade fudge. Fee charged.

Eau Galle Dam

U.S. Army Corps of Engineers, Eau Galle Lake, Spring Valley; 715-778-5562. From Hwy 29, turn onto Van Buren Road. Drive 1 mile to intersection of Co B. Cross B and follow park signs.

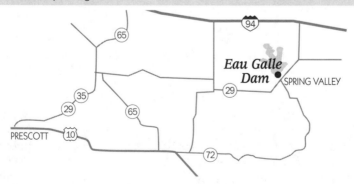

In 1943, famous architect Frank Lloyd Wright offered to design a new type

of village for Spring Valley, which was prone to repeated flooding. Wright proposed a town under one roof, or "mall" as they're known today. Had the folks taken him up on his offer, it would have been the first in existence by 13 years. Instead, the Army Corps of Engineers came up with a flood control plan, resulting in the construction of the Eau Galle Dam.

At 122' tall and 1,800' long, Eau Galle Dam is the largest earthen dam of this type in the Midwest. Completed in 1968, the project required more than 2 million cubic yards of rock and fill. The scenic overlook provides a great view of the dam and town below. The tall brick tower near the athletic fields is the remains of an early twentieth century iron ore smelter.

Eau Galle Lake offers picnicking, swimming, hiking, fishing, camping and nature programs. Day use fee charged.

> **Option:** If you're interested in the extraterrestrial, visit **Elmwood, the UFO capital of the world**. Located south of Spring Valley on Hwy 128, for some unknown reason this village of 800 folks attracts more than its share of visitors from outer space. Look for commemorative markers along the roadsides.

Southeastern Minnesota's Bluff Country

Explore two caves: Niagara Cave in Harmony, and Mystery Cave in Forestville State Park. From the Twin Cities, take Hwy 52 south to Harmony (approximately 140 miles).

Niagara Cave

Located 2 miles south of Harmony on Hwy 139; then 2 miles west on Niagara Cave Rd; 800-837-6606 or 507-886-6606; www.niagaracave.com

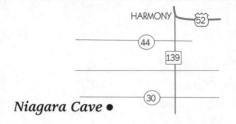

The Niagara Cave tour has it all: a roaring 60' waterfall, a 20' deep wishing well, a chapel room, stalactites, stalagmites, fossils, pitted limestone walls with 130' high ceilings, but absolutely no bats. You'll feel as though you're on a hike through the Grand Canyon—until the guide turns out the lights! Year-round temperature is 48 degrees, so bundle up and wear comfortable shoes. Gift shop, sluice trough and picnic facilities.

Guided tours Memorial Day through Labor Day, daily. Fee charged.

> **Options:** Don't miss a tour of **Austin's Angora Goats and Mohair**. Ada Austin's favorite book is *When I Am an Old Woman I Shall Wear Purple*. It's her guidebook for living, you might say, and the catalyst that changed her whole life. She promptly gave up a 20-year nursing career, painted her entire farm purple and bought a truckload of Angora goats—never mind she didn't know a thing about goats at the time. Ada is also the proud owner of three Navajo-Churro sheep. There are only 1,500 of these unique 4-horned animals in the U.S. You'll find Austin's 1 mile east of Harmony, off Hwy 52. Take the first gravel road to the left 1 mile and look for purple! Gift shop filled with everything "goat-made" including beautifully handcrafted Santas and angels, mohair blankets, socks, sweaters, goat milk soap, sausage and more. www.austinsmohair.com or 507-886-6731. Free farm tour. • About 700 Amish folks live in Harmony's surrounding rural area. Choose from several **tours** offered to learn more about their way of life: Michel's Amish Tours: 507-886-5392 or 800-752-6474. Fee charged. Amish Country Tours: 507-886-2303. Fee charged. R & M Amish Touring: 507-467-2128. 2-hour tour. Fee charged. • Travel the **Amish Buggy Byway** along Hwy 52 between Preston and Prosper (just north of the Iowa border). Many Amish farms and horse-drawn buggies along this route; farms dot the landscape.

Mystery Cave

> Forestville/Mystery Cave State Park; 507-937-3251; www.dnr.state.mn.us/state_parks/forestville_mystery_cave/index.html. From Hwy 16, follow Co 5 south to the cave; watch for signs.

Mystery Cave is Minnesota's longest cave. It has 13 miles of natural passages, two levels, clear blue pools, formations and fossils. Three guided tours to choose from: a one-hour tour with concrete ramps and walkways, a more rugged, two-hour tour (offered weekends only), or a 4-hour caving tour (1-week advance reservations required—Sa). Open Memorial Day–Labor Day 10 a.m.-5 p.m.; Spring and Fall, weekends only. Fee charged.

Options: Forestville State Park has 17 miles of trails through 3,000 acres of wooded ridges and valleys—Minnesota's most popular horse trails. Bring a rod and reel and try your luck in the trout streams. Camping available. • While you're in the park, take a self-guided tour through **Historic Forestville**. Once a thriving rural trade center of 100 residents, Forestville is now a living history museum. However, a fair word of warning: once you cross the bridge, you're back in 1899. The villagers think cameras are some type of music box! Open Memorial Day–Labor Day, closed Mondays. Sept. & Oct., open Sa–Su only; 507-765-2785; www.mnhs.org/places/sites/hf. State park permit required. Fee charged. • **Spring Valley** is only a few short miles west of Forestville on the junction of Hwys 63 & 16. Tour the historic 1876 Methodist Church Museum where Almanzo and Little House series author, Laura Ingalls Wilder attended Sunday services; 221 W Courtland St, 507-346-7659. Open Jun–Aug; wknds only Sep & Oct. Fee charged.

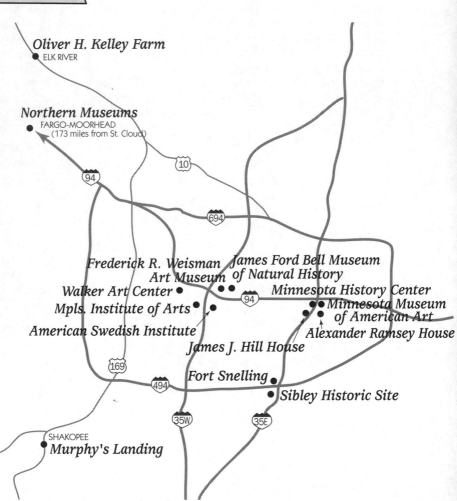

Oliver H. Kelley Farm
ELK RIVER

Northern Museums
FARGO-MOORHEAD
(173 miles from St. Cloud)

94

10

694

Frederick R. Weisman *James Ford Bell Museum*
Art Museum *of Natural History*
Walker Art Center ● *Minnesota History Center*
Mpls. Institute of Arts ● 94 *Minnesota Museum*
of American Art
American Swedish Institute *Alexander Ramsey House*
James J. Hill House
169 *Fort Snelling* ●
494 *Sibley Historic Site*
35W 35E
SHAKOPEE
Murphy's Landing

THEME: MUSEUMS, HISTORIC SITES & THE ARTS

Northern Museums

Twin Cities Area

*M*an's future is determined by how
well he learns from the past. Nowhere
are these lessons catalogued with more
passion than in our museums and art.
Many of the historical sites found in this
chapter provide opportunities for you to
partake in past events through the tal-
ented efforts of costumed interpreters.

Northern Museums

Originally settled by Scandinavian immigrants, the Red River Valley is one of the flattest land surfaces in North America, as well as one of the most fertile farming regions in the world. The metro area of Fargo-Moorhead and surrounding communities have a combined population of approximately 175,000 and an impressive number of museums and galleries.

Fargo-Moorhead Visitors' Center

2001 44th St (the "grain elevator" at exit 348 off of I-94), Fargo, ND; 800-235-7654 or 701-282-3653; www.fargomoorhead.org

Hollywood in Fargo? You betcha! The Red River Valley has its own Celebrity Walk of Fame located in the courtyard of the Visitors' Center. Garth Brooks, KISS, Neil Diamond, Aerosmith, George W. Bush, Dr. Ruth and many more star celebrities have their signatures, footprints and handprints set in cement. Pick up a free state map at the desk. Call for hours.

Bonanzaville

1351 W Main Ave, West Fargo, ND; 701-282-2822, www.bonanzaville.org

Tour 15 acres of historical buildings including a sod house, church, courthouse and country store. Also antique cars, airplanes and farm equipment. Costumed interpreters on hand to answer questions. Concessions. Wheelchair accessible. Call for hours. Fee charged.

Roger Maris Museum

3902 13th Ave S, West Acres Shopping Center, intersection of I-29 and 13th Ave, Fargo, ND; 701-282-2222; www.rogermarismuseum.com

Roger Maris—Fargo native and New York Yankee—hit 61 home runs during the 1961 season, besting Babe Ruth's longstanding record by one. Maris' uniforms, baseball equipment, awards and film footage of his last 12 homers from the 1961 season on exhibit at the West Acres Shopping Center. Concessions. Wheelchair accessible. Call for hours. Free.

Children's Museum at Yunker Farm

1201 28th Ave N, Fargo, ND; 701-232-6102; www.childrenmuseum-yunker.org

The Children's Museum at Yunker Farm features more than 50 hands-on exhibits, including a children's railroad and carousel. Self-guided tours. Closed Mondays. Wheelchair accessible. Fee charged.

Bergquist Pioneer Museum

11th St N, Moorhead, MN; 218-299-5520 (Clay County Museum)

Built in 1870, see Moorhead's oldest house still located on its original site. Seasonal tours.

Clay County Museum and Archives

202 1st Ave N, Moorhead, MN; 218-299-5520;
www.info.co.clay.mn.us/history/museum.htm

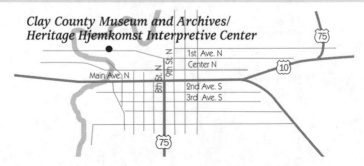

The Clay County Museum and Archives features historical aspects of Clay County communities with changing exhibits. Wheelchair accessible. Call for hours. Free.

Comstock House

506 8th St S, Moorhead, MN; 218-291-4211; www.mnhs.org/places/sites/ch

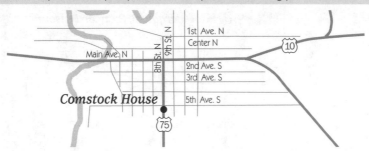

This 1882 Victorian Comstock House was the home of former state senator Solomon G. Comstock. Original furnishings, as well as the family's china, books and clothing. Open: Sa–Su, Tu & Th. Self-guided tours. Wheelchair accessible. Fee charged.

Heritage Hjemkomst Interpretive Center

202 1st Ave N, Moorhead, MN; 218-299-5511; www.hjemkomst-center.com

An award-winning documentary chronicles the construction of this 76' long, hand-built replica of a Viking ship and its 6,000-mile voyage across the Atlantic in 1982. The ship is on display at the Heritage Hjemkomst Interpretive Center.

Also on display is a replica of a Stavkirke Norwegian Church that dates back to the twelfth century. Long log columns are the central supports. Guided and self-guided tours. Wheelchair accessible. Fee charged.

Rourke Art Gallery and Museum

523 S 4th St (gallery) and 521 Main Ave (museum), Moorhead, MN; 218-236-8861

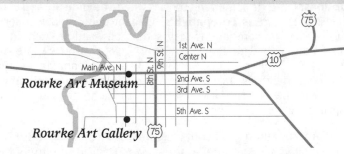

Housed in the 1880 historic Martinson home, the Rourke Art Gallery features regional artists. The museum (once the Moorhead post office) houses permanent collections of contemporary American, pre-Columbian, Hispanic, African and Native American art. Permanent and changing exhibits. Open: F–Su. Guided tours available. Wheelchair accessible. Fee charged.

Twin Cities Area

Alexander Ramsey House

265 S Exchange St, downtown St. Paul (located off Ramsey St, 1 blk south of W 7th St); 651-296-8760 or 651-296-0100 (reservations recommended);www.mnhs.org/places/sites/arh

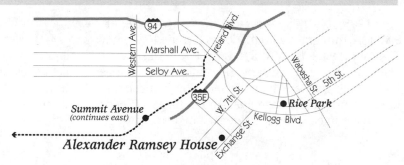

The 1872 Victorian home of Alexander and Anna Ramsey is located in historic Irvine Park. Ramsey was Minnesota's first territorial governor, and the second state governor. Costumed interpreters guide visitors through rooms with marble fireplaces, crystal chandeliers, walnut woodwork and the latest in labor-saving devices of the day. Stop in the kitchen for a cookie, then visit the museum shop in the carriage house. Open year-round. Call for hours, vary by season. Fee charged.

Options: Lunch is something special when you dine at the 1870 Victorian mansion known as **Forepaugh's**. Elegant decor and wonderful French cuisine. The desserts are as they should be—sinfully rich and delicious. Main floor pub with fireplace. 651-224-5606 or www.forepaughs.com. Lunch—$$. Dinner—$$–$$$. • Since you're probably in a very mansion-like mood right now, take a drive along **Historic Summit Avenue**. Give a wave to the Governor if you see him, as his home is among these magnificent architectural wonders.

NOTE: Famous author F. Scott Fitzgerald's birthplace is the apartment building located at 481 Laurel Avenue—very near in proximity to the mansions, but not near in grandeur. There's a life-size statue of Fitzgerald in Rice Park.

American Swedish Institute

2600 Park Ave, Minneapolis; 612-871-4907 or www.americanswedishinst.org

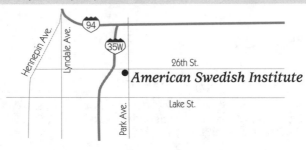

The 1908 castle-like structure was the home of Swan J. Turnblad, a Swedish immigrant who made his fortune in the newspaper business. The 33-room castle is now a Swedish American cultural center. Elaborate woodcarvings and plasterwork, antique furnishings, 11 tile stoves and a Swedish glassware exhibit. Coffee shop, gift shop and bookstore (items in English and all the Scandinavian languages). Special programs and concerts. Open year-round, call for hours. Fee charged.

Fort Snelling

Located between the Mississippi River and the Twin Cities Int'l Airport at the junction of Hwys 5 & 55, St. Paul; 612-726-1171 or www.mnhs.org/places/sites/hfs.

Restored historic Fort Snelling opens its gates and welcomes you to 19th-century frontier life. Talk with soldiers who grumble about farm chores. Help with the laundry using a washboard and lye soap. Meet a Dakota trader's wife or have tea with Mrs. Snelling. Watch the blacksmith at his forge. Learn how to shoulder a musket, mend clothes and scrape a hide. In short, partake in everyday life at the fort. May–Oct, open daily. Call for off-season schedule. Exhibits, films and gift shop. Daily cannon shoot. Wheelchair accessible. Fee charged.

Frederick R. Weisman Art Museum

333 E River Rd (University of Minnesota campus), Minneapolis; 612-625-9494; www.weisman.umn.edu

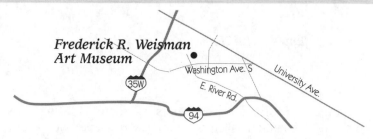

Find the only odd-shaped, stainless steel-wrapped building in the Twin Cities and you'll have found the Weisman. Known for its bold sculptures, contemporary paintings and imaginative exhibits. Put your ear to a door and do some legal eavesdropping at an exhibit simulating a hotel hallway. Closed Mondays. Gift shop. Wheelchair accessible. Free.

James Ford Bell Museum of Natural History

10 Church St (University of Minnesota campus), Minneapolis; 612-624-7083 or www.bellmuseum.org

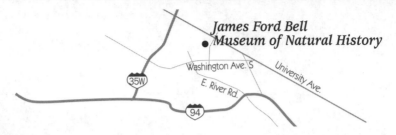

The James Ford Bell Museum has hands-on exhibits for children and adults. Lifelike animal and plant displays. Closed Mondays. Wheelchair accessible. Fee charged.

James J. Hill House

240 Summit Ave (½ blk. west of the Cathedral), St. Paul; 651-297-2555 or www.mnhs.org/places/sites/jjhh

The 1891 James J. Hill House has 4 floors, 42 rooms, 22 fireplaces, 13 bathrooms, a 100' reception hall, a skylit art gallery, carved woodwork and stained glass. At the time, this massive stone building was the largest and most expensive private home in the state. A guided tour tells about owner James J. Hill's life and his transportation empire—the Great Northern Railway. Open year-round, reservations recommended. Wheelchair accessible. Fee charged.

Minneapolis Institute of Arts

2400 3rd Ave S, Minneapolis; 612-870-3131 or 888-MIA-ARTS; www.artsMIA.org

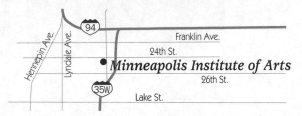

The Minneapolis Institute of Arts houses the nation's best Asian art, as well as more than 100,000 other objects. The collection represents artistic traditions and treasures spanning 5,000 years. Closed Mondays. Restaurant, coffee shop, gift shop. Wheelchair accessible. Free except for special exhibits.

Minnesota History Center

345 Kellogg Blvd W; on the corner of Kellogg and John Ireland Blvds in downtown St. Paul; 888-727-8386 or 651-259-3000; www.mnhs.org/historycenter

The state's events come alive at the Minnesota History Center. Animated displays, hands-on exhibits—you'll have so much fun, you won't even realize you're in a history center. Open year-round Tu–Su. Also open Mondays during summer months. Restaurant, gift shop, library, genealogy collection. Wheelchair accessible. Free.

> **Option:** The **Minnesota State Capitol** is within walking distance of the Minnesota History Center. See the four golden horses, soaring domes, arches and columns, statues and symbolic murals. All galleries and legislative hearings are open to the public during sessions. www.mnhs.org/places/sites/msc or 651-296-2881. Open daily, year-round, hours vary by season. Free guided tours. Restaurant. Wheelchair accessible.

Minnesota Museum of American Art

50 W Kellogg Blvd, St. Paul; 651-266-1030 or www.mmaa.org

Minnesota Museum of American Art

The Minnesota Museum of American Art houses paintings by well-known artists such as Thomas Hart Benton, Childe Hassam and Grant Wood. Closed Mondays. Wheelchair accessible. Free.

The Landing (formerly Murphy's)

2187 E Hwy 101, Shakopee, MN (located 1 mile east of Shakopee on Hwy 101); 763-694-7784 or www.threeriversparkdistrict.org/outdoor_ed/murphys_landing

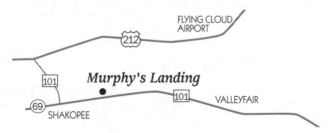

At The Landing, you'll journey from the early days of the fur trade era to a bustling 19th century village. Hear about the daily life of the families who settled in the Minnesota River Valley from costumed interpreters. Take a ride on a horse-drawn trolley and watch craft demonstrations. Music and entertainment daily. Gift shop and restaurant. Open May–Oct. Fee charged.

Option: If you happen to be in the area during August and September, check out the **Renaissance Festival**, located 3 miles south of Shakopee on Hwy 169. This is sixteenth century pageantry combined with rowdy fun! Full-contact armored jousting, human combat chess, damsels in distress and nobles of the royal court. Wander the authentic village marketplace where close to 300 artisans hawk their hand-crafted goods. Gnaw on a turkey drumstick while enjoying the antics of comedians, Puke and Snot. Magicians, jugglers, musicians and more. Aug–Sep, weekends only. Free parking. Wheelchair accessible. Fee charged. 800-966-8215.

Oliver H. Kelley Farm

15788 Kelley Farm Rd, Elk River; 763-441-6896 or www.mnhs.org/places/sites/ohkf

Oliver H. Kelley Farm

Try your hand at 1800s farming at the 189-acre Oliver H. Kelley Farm. Costumed interpreters won't mind if you want to take a turn plowing with oxen or threshing the grain. Partake in the household chores of churning butter, washing laundry with a scrub board and cooking on a wood stove. Nature trails follow the Mississippi River through woods and restored prairies. The visitor center features a bookstore, videos and exhibits. Open May–Sep. Call for hours. Wheelchair accessible. Fee charged.

Sibley Historic Site

1357 Sibley Memorial Hwy (Hwy 13 northeast of the Mendota bridge and across the river from Fort Snelling), Mendota; 651-452-1596 or www.mnhs.org/places/sites/shs

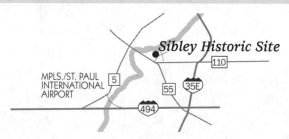

The Sibley Historic Site is Minnesota's oldest European-American settlement. Through costumed interpreters, learn about the life of Henry Sibley, the state's first governor. Explore two 1830s limestone houses, a fur company cold store and the Jean Baptiste Faribault Hotel. Open May–Oct. Fee charged, free for children ages 5 and under.

Walker Art Center

1750 Hennepin Ave, Minneapolis; 612-375-7600; www.walkerart.org

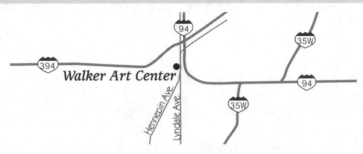

The newly expanded art museum features permanent collections of 20th century paintings, sculptures, video art, and photographs, as well as two restaurants by Wolfgang Puck, gift shop, library, state-of-the-art theater and cinema. Check out Gallery 9 on their Website The works of more than 100 artists have been featured here since 1997. Free gallery and architecture tours (with paid gallery admission) Thurs–Sun. Garden tours Sat & Sun. The gallery is closed on Mon. Call for a schedule of upcoming live performances and events. Fee charged. Free admission Thurs evenings and the first Sat of each month. Free for children age 12 and under.

The Walker Art Center is also home to the adjoining 11-acre Minneapolis Sculpture Garden with its Spoonbridge and Cherry Fountain. The garden is open daily 6 a.m.–midnight. Free admission.

Forepaugh's (pg. 108)

Minnesota History Center (pg. 111)

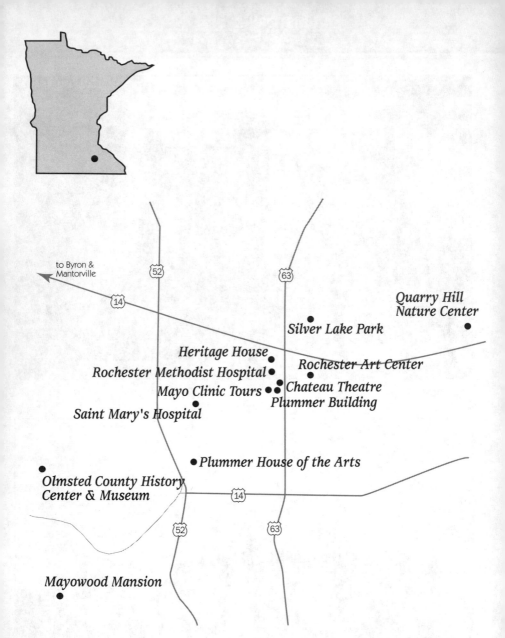

to Byron &
Mantorville

Quarry Hill
Nature Center

Silver Lake Park

Heritage House

Rochester Methodist Hospital

Rochester Art Center

Mayo Clinic Tours

Chateau Theatre

Plummer Building

Saint Mary's Hospital

Plummer House of the Arts

Olmsted County History
Center & Museum

Mayowood Mansion

THEME: ROCHESTER

Touring Rochester's Highlights

Rochester
NEXT RIGHT

*R*ochester is home to 80,000 people, 30,000 giant Canada geese, the world-renowned Mayo Medical Center, 8 golf courses (do doctors live here or what?), an extensive parks system, the largest IBM complex under one roof, sports, theater, an international airport, topnotch restaurants and shopping. Named one of the three most livable cities in America by Money Magazine, Rochester has got it all!

For more information, call the Rochester Convention and Visitors Bureau: 800-634-8277 or 507-288-4331; www.rochestercvb.org.

Touring Rochester's Highlights

From the Twin Cities, drive south approximately 90 miles on Hwy 52.

Mayo Clinic Tours

Downtown Rochester. The Mayo Building occupies a square block between 1st and 2nd Sts SW and 2nd and 3rd Aves SW; 507-538-0440; www.mayo.edu/mcr/helpful_info.html

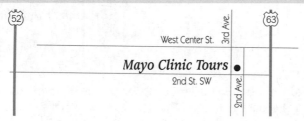

Established in 1889, the Mayo Clinic is the world's largest private medical center. It occupies 47 buildings—a space equal to two and a half times larger than the Mall of America. The facility registers nearly a quarter million patients each year and has a worldwide reputation for innovation and surgical excellence. Take a 90-minute tour of the clinic M–F; call for times. Movie in Judd Auditorium. Free admission.

> **Option:** The **Art and Architecture Tour** includes the works of Miro, Calder, Milles and Warhol. Judd Auditorium, M–F. 507-284-1545. Free.

Saint Mary's Hospital & Rochester Methodist Hospital

Saint Mary's: 1216 2nd St SW; 507-255-5123; www.mayoclinic.org/saintmaryshospital/
Rochester Methodist: 201 W Center St; 507-266-7890; www.mayoclinic.org/methodisthospital/

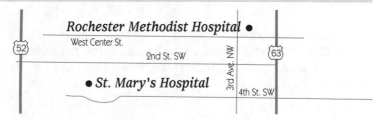

Both St. Mary's and Rochester Methodist are part of the Mayo Medical Center network. Self-guided tours, 8 a.m.–8 p.m.; tour brochures available at the Information Desk.

Plummer Building

2nd Ave and 2nd St SW (across from the Mayo Building); 507-284-8294

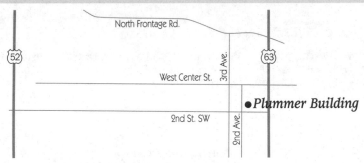

Housed in the tower of the Plummer Building, the 56-bell Rochester Carillon covers a 4½ octave range. The largest bell weighs over 7,800 pounds. Third floor tours of the original offices of founding Drs. William J. and Charles H. Mayo. Open M–F. Free.

Mayowood Mansion

3720 Mayowood Rd SW; 507-282-9447; www.olmstedhistory.com/mayowood.htm

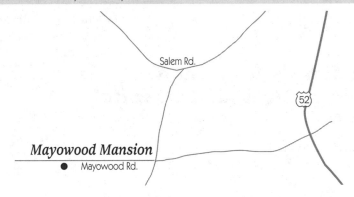

The gorgeous, 48-room Mayowood Mansion was home to three generations of Mayos. Furniture, antiques and Mayo family mementos. Expansive grounds, beautiful gardens. Tours: May through mid-Oct Call for days and hours. Fee charged.

Plummer House of the Arts

1091 Plummer Ln. SW; 507-328-2525;
www.ci.rochester.mn.us/departments/park/facilities/plummerhouse

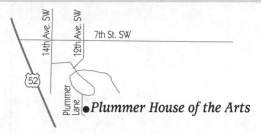

Plummer House of the Arts

The 49-room Tudor mansion was the home of Dr. Henry S. Plummer, the innovator credited for the Mayo's lift systems, pneumatic tubes and accessible medical records. Plummer installed many state-of-the-art gadgets of the time in his home, such as a central vacuum, garage door openers, a gas furnace and an intercom system. Eleven landscaped acres, formal gardens, bird trail, quarry and water tower. Grounds open year-round. Tours Jun–Aug, Wed and the first and third Sundays. Fee charged.

Quarry Hill Nature Center

Quarry Hill Nature Center, 701 Silver Creek Rd NE (located on the northeast edge of Rochester. Take Co 22 to Silver Creek Rd); 507-281-6114; www.qhnc.org

Quarry Hill Nature Center

The Quarry Hill Nature Center has five miles of trails covering 270 acres. Interactive displays and exhibits including a 1,700-gallon native fish aquarium, hundreds of mounted animals and a life-sized *T. Rex* skull model. Open year-round, daily. Free.

Chateau Theatre

15 1st St SW; 800-634-8277 or 507-288-4331 (Rochester Convention and
Visitors Bureau)

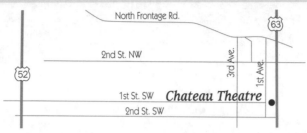

Built in 1927, the elegant old theater is now home to Barnes & Noble
Bookstore and Starbucks Cafe. A 1994 refurbishing maintained the
Chateau's unique "French village" decor of interior balconies and turrets.
Open daily, year-round.

Silver Lake Park

North Broadway; 800-634-8277 or 507-288-4331 (Rochester Convention and
Visitors Bureau)

Over 30,000 giant Canada Geese descend on Rochester in November, and
more than half make Silver Lake Park their winter home. Outdoor pool,
skate park, playground equipment, picnic facilities. Bike, paddleboat and
canoe rental Memorial Day–Labor Day, daily.

Heritage House

Downtown Rochester in the Town Square Central Park; 800-634-8277 or 507-288-4331 (Rochester Convention and Visitors Bureau)

Heritage House offers a glimpse of what life was like for a middle-class Midwestern family a century ago. Open June–Aug, Tu, Th & Su. Fee charged.

Olmsted County History Center & Museum

1195 W Circle Dr SW; 507-282-9447;www.olmstedhistory.com

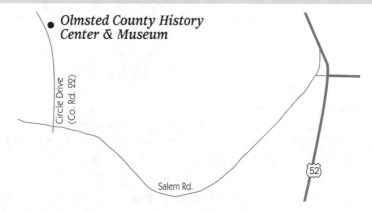

Learn the story behind Rochester's rise as a global leader in health care through exhibits at the Olmsted County History Center & Museum. Open year-round. Closed M & Su and all major holidays

Explore the 1862 William Dee Log Cabin, Hadley Valley School House and the George Stoppel Farm (est. 1856). Open Memorial Day–Labor Day. Fee charged.

Rochester Art Center

40 Civic Center Dr SE; 507-282-8629

The Rochester Art Center features fine arts and crafts as well as changing exhibits. On Thursday evenings the Art Center sponsors a series of videos showcasing artists and their work. Open year-round; Th—free; Tu–W, F–Su—fee charged.

Near Rochester: Byron & Mantorville

BYRON:
The **Oxbow Park & Zollman Zoo** (15 minute drive from Rochester)—take Hwy 14 west to Byron, turn north on Co 5, go 3 miles, watch for signs. Oxbow Park and Zollman Zoo offer wooded hiking trails, a picturesque stream with bridges, playground equipment, picnic facilities and nature center. 507-775-2451 or www.co.olmsted.mn.us. Fee charged for zoo.

MANTORVILLE:
Mantorville is 17 miles from Rochester. Take Hwy 14 west to Kasson, then go 3 miles north on Hwy 57; www.mantorville.com. A town of 800, **Historic Mantorville** features a covered bridge, antiques and gift shops, fine dining and plenty of nostalgic charm.

Once a stagecoach stop, the 1856 **Hubbell House** restaurant has served such celebrities as Mickey Mantle, Dwight Eisenhower and Roy Rogers. Wonderful food, Civil War-era decor. On the main drag in Mantorville. 507-635-2331or www.hubbellhouserestaurant.com. Closed M—$$.

Let your nose lead you to **The Chocolate Shoppe**. They make their own sinfully delicious chocolate and caramel confections right on the premises. Try their chocolate-covered potato chips. They also sell 40 different flavors of jelly beans, taffy and other candies. On Main Street, on the corner across from the Hubbell House. Closed M. 507-635-5814.

Once a grocery store, **Memorabilia** now stocks the meat and produce coolers with antique spice cans and glassware. Nice displays featuring full china sets and antique stemware. You'll feel as if you've been invited to a formal dinner party. Furniture and more. Memorabilia is next to the Opera House. 507-635-5419.

Make a night of it and see a live performance by **The Mantorville Theatre Company** in the Historic Opera House. Box office opens one hour before showtime. Mid-Jun through Sep, F–Su. 507-635-5420 or www.mantorvillain.com. Fee charged.

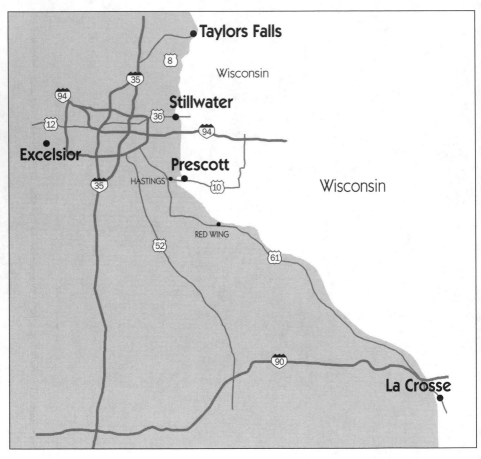

THEME: *Romantic Getaways*

ROMANTIC GETAWAYS

14

*T*he whole world loves a lover, and that must go double for a couple in love! To keep the fires of passion burning, stoke them often with the romantic getaways found in this chapter. Each enchanting trip is filled with picturesque small towns, lazy strolls, candlelit evenings and plenty of opportunity to romance the one you love.

Taylors Falls

Taylors Falls is less than an hour's drive from the Twin Cities. Take I-94 east
to Hwy 95 north. Taylors Falls Chamber of Commerce: 800-447-4958 or
651-645-6315; www.taylorsfallschamber.org.

Old Jail Bed & Breakfast

349 Government St, Taylors Falls; 651-465-3112; www.oldjail.com

Spend a weekend with the old "ball and chain" in the historic 1884 Jail
Cottage, but don't worry—the hearty breakfasts are a delicious far cry
from bread and water. You're expected, however, to put up with such
things as spaciousness, privacy and beautiful views. If that sounds like
your kind of torture, reserve a cell for yourself and a mate—$$–$$$.

Interstate State Park

Taylors Falls on Hwy 8 along the St. Croix River; 651-465-5711 or
www.dnr.state.mn.us/state_parks/interstate/index.html

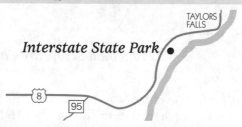

Pack a lunch and hike the 4 miles of trails in Minnesota's second-oldest
state park. Take your time exploring the numerous glacial potholes—one
is 60' deep and considered the deepest pothole in the world! If you're a
rock climber, you'll be in good company as many come to scale
Interstate's challenging cliffs.

Tired of walking? Then take a riverboat excursion, rent a canoe or just park
yourself on a nearby 1.1 billion-year-old boulder and soak up the pulsing
green landscape. State Park permit required.

Folsom House

272 Government St, Taylors Falls; 651-465-3125;
www.mnhs.org/places/sites/fh/index.html; Angel Hill Historic District

Take a guided tour of lumber baron W.H.C. Folsom's home. The 1855 Greek Revival house has colorful rooms, wood floors and a cheery New England feel. Open Memorial Day through mid-Oct. Closed Tu. Fee charged.

Option: After your tour, do a little sightseeing on your own. Walk or drive past the many other restored homes in the **Angel Hill Historic District**.

Franconia Sculpture Park

29836 St Croix Trail, Franconia (on Hwy 8); 651-257-6668; www.franconia.org

Experienced artists from all over the world (and those still wet behind the ears) bring their own unique vision to life at the 16-acre Franconia Sculpture Park. Meet the sculptors and watch them work during the summer months. Open daily: dawn–dusk.

Option: In nearby Osceola, Wisconsin, hop a vintage diesel or steam-powered train for a ride through the rolling hills of the Dairy State, or choose a longer excursion to Marine-on-St. Croix, Minnesota. Get off and stretch the legs in this captivating river town. April–Oct. Weekends and holidays only. Call **Scenic Osceola & St. Croix Railway**, 800-711-2591 or 651-228-0263 or visit www.trainride.org for schedule and fees.

Stillwater

Directions: A short 20-minute drive from the Twin Cities. Take I-94 east to Hwy 95 north. Another option is Hwy 36 east. Stillwater Chamber of Commerce: 651-439-4001; www.ilovestillwater.com.

Aamodt's Hot Air Balloon Ride

6428 Manning Ave N, 651-351-0101 or 866-3HOT-AIR (866-546-8247); (five miles east of Hwy 36, left ½ mile.); www.aamodtsballoons.com

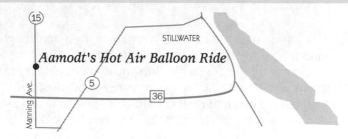

What could be more romantic than floating away together in one of Aamodt's hot air balloons? Experience this peaceful way to travel the scenic river valley while your pilot points out interesting sights. Ninety minute ride departs 3 miles west of Stillwater at Aamodt's Apple Farm, then returns for a champagne toast. Fee charged.

Options: Once back in Stillwater, take a leisurely stroll along the riverfront. Watch the lift bridge in action, enjoy the gardens and shop the boutiques. Spend a pleasant hour or two dining on the open deck at the **Freight House Restaurant**, found along the river's edge—$–$$. 651-439-5718; www.fhstillwater.com • Board the **Stillwater Trolley** for a 45-minute narrated tour featuring the city's lumberjack days. A drive by Stillwater's beautifully restored homes is included on the trolley route. Open May–Oct, daily. Board at the Freight House. 651-430-0352; www.stillwatertrolley.com. Fee charged. • **Gondola St. Croix**, Stillwater public dock, 651-439-1783 or www.gondolaromantica.com. Nothing spells romance like an Italian serenade while gliding down the St. Croix nestled in a gondola from Venice. Gondola St. Croix offers a glimpse into the Venetian world as it was a millennium ago. Bring a picnic lunch or have them arrange something special for you. Rides range from 25 minutes to 1 hour and seat up to six. Solo violinist or ensemble available. Summer evenings daily, by appt. only. Fee charged.

Aurora Staples Inn

303 N 4th St; 651-351-1187; www.aurorastaplesinn.com

Stillwater is an antiquer's paradise. With so many interesting shops to poke around in, it's a real challenge to visit them all. Thank heavens you reserved a room at the Aurora Staples Inn and don't have to try to fit everything into one day. The 1892 Victorian mansion overlooks the St. Croix River. A wraparound porch, formal gardens, an open oak staircase and five rooms with private baths, whirlpools and fireplaces. Full breakfast—$$$–$$$$.

James A. Mulvey Residence Inn

622 W Churchill St; 651-430-8008 or 800-820-8008; www.jamesmulveyinn.com

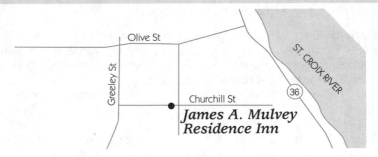

Built in 1878, the James A. Mulvey Residence Inn features 1.5 acres of gardens. Afternoon sweet treats and tea, 4-course breakfast served on sun porch or formal dining room. Each of the seven rooms decorated in a different motif ranging from period Victorian to Southwest. Double whirlpools, fireplaces, balconies—$$–$$$$.

Lowell Inn

102 N 2nd St, Stillwater; 651-439-1100; www.lowellinn.com

After you've had a chance to freshen up a bit, it's time to think about those dinner plans. *Gourmet Magazine* voted the Lowell Inn the most romantic dining experience in the Twin Cities. The Lowell Inn offers three distinct and beautiful dining settings, from very formal (The George Washington Room) to alfresco. The Matterhorn Room serves Swiss Fondue and fantastic wines. Rooms available—$$$–$$$$.

NOTE: Stillwater offers many bed and breakfast accommodations as well as motels. Call the Stillwater Chamber of Commerce for more information: 651-439-4001; www.ilovestillwater.com.

Excelsior

Excelsior is located about 20 minutes west of the Twin Cities on Hwy 7. Visit Excelsior's website at www.southlake-excelsiorchamber.com.

Antiquity Rose

429 2nd St, Excelsior; 952-474-2661

If you've never been to Excelsior before, you're in for a real treat. The town has wonderful shops and gardens, tons of antiques and a nice breeze off Lake Minnetonka, to boot. So after you've had a chance to explore a bit, wander into the Antiquity Rose for lunch. Homemade breads, matzo ball

133

soup and even tuna hot dish, if you're in the mood. Love the old-fashioned china you're eating on? Then cut a deal with the owner to purchase it. Nearly everything at Antiquity Rose is for sale, even the chair you're sitting on. Open M–Sa. Wheelchair accessible—$.

Steamboat Minnehaha

Water St; 952-474-4801 (ticket office) or 952-474-2115; www.steamboatminnehaha.org

Enjoy the scenery aboard the restored 1905 steamboat *Minnehaha* as she travels across Lake Minnetonka to Wayzata. Get off and look around or return to Excelsior. Operates mid-May through mid-Oct, Sa and Su. Board at the dock on Water St. Purchase tickets at the museum office across the street from the dock.—$.

Excelsior Streetcar Line

Water St; 952-474-2115; www.trolleyride.org

If boats aren't for you, then take a 1-mile ride on Car No. 78—one of the oldest operating, museum-quality trolleys in the country. The 10-minute ride aboard the beautifully restored yellow streetcar is a journey back to the turn of the century. Catch the streetcar at Water Street. May through Oct; Th, Sa, Su and holidays. Fee charged.

The Old Log Theater

5185 Meadville St; 952-474-5951 or 866-653-5641 ext 4328; www.oldlog.com

As the sun slips below the horizon, the lakeside trees come alive with sparkling white lights. End the day with a romantic dinner for two and a live performance at The Old Log Theater—the oldest continuously running theater in the country. Wheelchair accessible. Call for reservations.

Prescott, Wisconsin

Prescott is approximately 30 miles from the Twin Cities. Take Hwy 61 south, then turn east on Hwy 10. Prescott Area Chamber of Commerce: 715-262-3284 or www.prescottwi.com.

Prescott is Wisconsin's oldest river town and one of its most romantic. Stroll the charming downtown shops and cafes on Broad Street.

Funkie Gardens

618 Pearl St; 715-262-5593. Take Hwy 10 E, turn right on Pearl St. Travel 5 blocks, gardens are on the left; www.funkiegardens.com

Known for unique perennials, Funkie Gardens' gorgeous display gardens feature over 600 varieties of plants surrounding a pre-Civil War-era home. Open May–Sep; closed M & Tu.

Welcome & Heritage Center

Corner of Broadway and Hwy 10 (next to the bridge); 715-262-3284 or www.pressenter.com/~whctr

Stop in at the Welcome & Heritage Center for free maps and information on the Great River Road and the charming Wisconsin Rustic Road. For those interested in history, the center is a great place to begin Prescott's Historic Walking Tour of fourteen sites, including Mercord Mill Park (at the confluence of the St. Croix and Mississippi Rivers) and the 1923 Vertical-Lift Bridge Gearhouse.

The Arbor Inn Bed & Breakfast

434 N Court St; 888-262-1090 or 715-262-2222; www.thearborinn.com

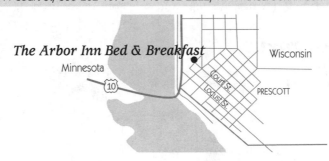

The 1902 mission style home is loaded with English country charm, right down to its quilts and breakfast porches with grapevines. Four rooms with private baths; whirlpools for 2; hot tub under the stars with a river view. Offers wellness massages and a full breakfast—$$$–$$$$.

La Crosse, Wisconsin

Julia Belle Swain Steamboat Cruise

La Crosse, Wisconsin is approximately 140 miles from the Twin Cities. Drive south on Hwy 61 and cross the Mississippi River into La Crosse. Board the Julia Belle Swain at Riverside Park in La Crosse; 800-815-1005 or 608-784-4882; www.juliabelle.com. La Crosse website: www.explorelacrosse.com

Nothing's quite as romantic as a river cruise aboard a vintage steamboat. There's just something so irresistibly enchanting about that paddlewheel and all the white gingerbread trim. Take your lemonade or tea on the open deck or relax with a cool drink from the bar in the richly appointed dining salon.

The Julia Belle Swain is one of only five authentic steam-powered passenger vessels still in operation on the Mississippi River. She has an operating steam calliope with antique keyboard and 1915 engines. She's also become quite a celebrity, having appeared in several motion pictures.

Overnight and extended cruises offered, as well as shorter brunch, lunch and dinner trips. Some meals and snacks included. Call or visit the website for more information.

Julia Belle Swain Steamboat Cruise (pg. 137)

Funkie Gardens (pg. 135)

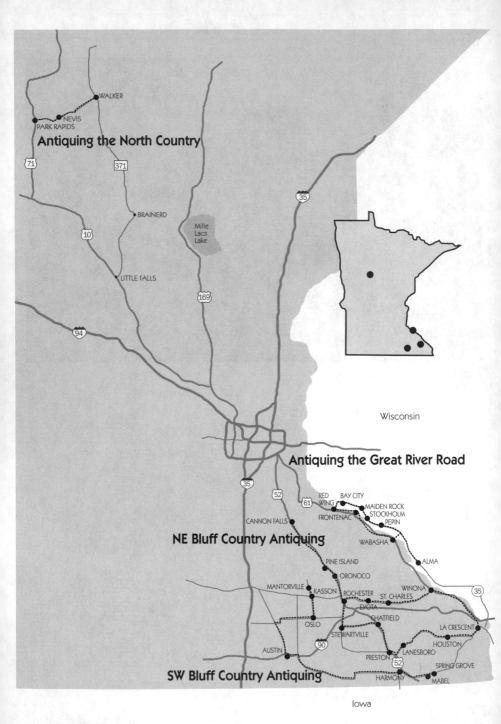

Antiquing the North Country

WALKER
NEVIS
PARK RAPIDS

71   371

BRAINERD

Mille
Lacs
Lake

10

LITTLE FALLS

169

94

Wisconsin

Antiquing the Great River Road

RED WING   BAY CITY
35   52   61   MAIDEN ROCK
FRONTENAC   STOCKHOLM
PEPIN

CANNON FALLS

NE Bluff Country Antiquing

WABASHA

ALMA

PINE ISLAND
ORONOCO

MANTORVILLE   KASSON   ROCHESTER   WINONA
ST. CHARLES   35
EYOTA
OSLO   CHATFIELD
STEWARTVILLE   LA CRESCENT
HOUSTON
AUSTIN   90   LANESBORO
PRESTON   SPRING GROVE
SW Bluff Country Antiquing   52
HARMONY   MABEL

Iowa

THEME: SMALL TOWN ANTIQUING

SW Bluff Country Antiquing

*I*t's been said the best antiques are old friends, but that doesn't mean you can't fall in love with a primitive pine bench or a piece of colorful majolica. This chapter shares some of Minnesota's best spots for antiquing in small towns that are as charming and vintage as the wares they sell.

Antiquing the North Country

For antiques lovers, it's as much about the hunt as it is the purchase. A day spent in these small town gems is surely one you'll treasure.

Park Rapids

Park Rapids' old-fashioned confectionaries, soda fountains, charming shops and vintage Main Street is enough to make any antiques lover swoon. For more information about the city and surrounding communities, contact the Park Rapids Chamber of Commerce at 800-247-0054 or 218-732-4112 or www.parkrapids.com.

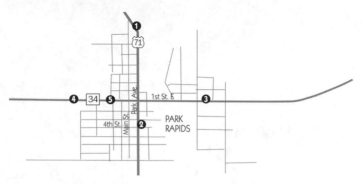

1. **Park Rapids Trading Post**, 19866 U.S. Hwy 71, Park Rapids; 218-732-0251. Open Apr–Nov. Antiques and used household goods.

2. **Rich's Antiques**, 409 Park Ave S, Park Rapids; 218-732-3949. Open daily. General line.

3. **Six-Toed Cat Antiques**, 808 E 1st St, Park Rapids; 218-732-8919; Open May–Dec, M–Sa. Specializes in American and European art and furniture. www.sixtoedcatantiques.com

4. **Summerset Outdoor Flea Market**, 17770 Hwy 34, Park Rapids; 218-732-5570. Open Memorial Day–Labor Day, Th, weather permitting.

5. **Toys for Boys**, 4 blocks west of Hwy 71 on Hwy 34, Park Rapids; 218-732-5668. Specialties include '40s and '50s era collectibles. James Dean, Marilyn Monroe, Betty Boop and more.

Option: Summerhill Farm, Hwy 71 North, Park Rapids; 218-732-3865.; www.summerhill-farm.com. Seven unique gift shops featured inside a barn, stable, carriage house, treehouse and more. There's also the Sun Porch for lunch and delicious desserts. Open daily mid-May to mid-September. • Take a candle factory tour at **Candles!** You can dip your own candle or shop for unique candles and gifts at factory prices. Located 4 miles north of Park Rapids on Hwy 71; 218-732-7703. Free tours Tu & Th at noon. Open daily.

Nevis

Nevis is midpoint on the 27-mile long Heartland Trail, Minnesota's first rail-to-trail system. The paved trail winds through woods, offering excellent birding and gorgeous lake views. Nevis also boasts the world's largest tiger muskie...statue, that is.

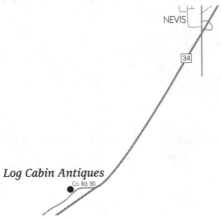

Log Cabin Antiques, 21290 Co Rd 80 N, Nevis; 218-732-9863. Only open in the summer—call for hours.

Walker

Located on the southwest side of Leech Lake (one of Minnesota's largest lakes), Walker offers scenic beauty, magnificent hiking, biking, horseback trails and great shopping. Bargain hunt at their fantastic "crazy day" sales (held monthly, summer only). www.walkermn.com.

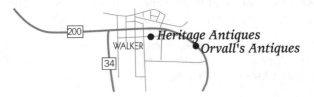

Orvall's Antiques, 514 Minnesota Ave W, Walker; 218-547-2966. Seasonal, M–Sa.

Heritage Antiques, Village Square Building, 5th & Minnesota, Walker; 218-547-3501. Furniture, accessories.

Options: • Relax with a cruise on beautiful Leech Lake. **Coborn's Leech Lake Cruises** offers daily cruises, full bar and light dining. Find them on Hwy 371 between Walker and Northern Lights Casino; 218-547-4150.

Antiquing the Great River Road

Voted one of the ten most scenic drives in America, traveling the Great River Road (Hwy 35) offers more than unparalleled beauty—it's also a great place to hunt antiques. This 100-mile trip crisscrosses Minnesota and Wisconsin. And although it doesn't cover every single antiques shop, it does treat you to many goodies not always on the beaten path. www.wigreatriverroad.org or www.mississippi-river.org

Red Wing

Hwy 61 south from the Twin Cities approximately 50 miles; www.redwing.org

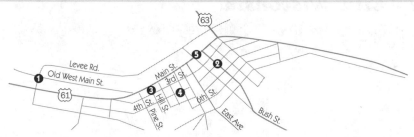

This pretty river town is home to Red Wing Shoes and the birthplace of Red Wing Pottery. For more information, visit the Red Wing Visitors and Convention Bureau (800-498-3444 or 651-385-5934), located behind the St. James Hotel in the Amtrak/Greyhound Depot.

1. **Pottery Place Antiques**, 2000 Old W Main St (3rd floor of Pottery Outlet Center); 651-388-7765; www.potteryplaceantiques.com. Open daily. Maintains a large pottery and furniture line.

2. **Al's Antique Mall**, 512 Plum St (one block off Hwy 61). Open daily; 651-388-0572 or 888-388-0572; Features just about everything. 12,000 square feet.

3. **Hill Street Antiques**, 212 Hill St (3 blks east of Al's Antique Mall across from the Kwik Trip). Open daily in the summer, Sa & Su or by chance on weekdays in the winter; 651-388-0736. Specializes in Red Wing dinnerware, art pottery and stoneware—over 5,000 pieces.

4. **Teahouse Antiques**, 703 W 4th St (2 blks off Hwy 61—turn at Randy's Restaurant). Open daily since 1966. 651-388-3669. General line.

5. Memory Maker Antiques, 415 Main St (Hwy 61). Open daily; 651-385-5914. 6,000 square feet of walnut, oak and pine furniture, glassware, and the largest selection of tools in the area.

Options: Although the original Red Wing pottery business closed in 1969, the **Red Wing Stoneware Company** bought the reproduction rights and still uses some of the original molds. Open daily, watch potters at work through a window in the showroom. Located on Hwy 61 in the industrial park at the west end of town. 800-352-4877 or 651-388-4610. • The **Cannon Valley Trail** connects Red Wing, Welch and Cannon Falls. www.cannonvalleytrail.com. More than 20 miles of scenic hiking and biking. Located 1 block off Hwy 61 on Old W Main St & Bench St. Parking lot with facilities. • Restored to its Victorian splendor, the 19th-century **St. James Hotel** offers pampered overnight stays, fine dining, lunches on the veranda, an English pub and courtyard shopping. 406 Main St; 800-252-1875 or 651-388-2846; www.st-james-hotel.com.

Bay City, Wisconsin

Hwy 63. Turn east on Hwy 35 and follow to Bay City. Watch for bald eagles along the way!

Oldstuff, Hwy 35 (renovated gas station at the east end of town). Nice folks with a lot of knowledge of the business and local area. Open year-round by chance. If the sign's out, they're open. Glassware, primitives, collectibles, yard finds. 715-594-3229.

Option: For the sweetest blueberries and a valley view that won't quit, stop in at **Rush River Produce**. Pick your own, or buy already picked. Look for the sign on Hwy 35, turn north onto Co A and follow signs. Also raspberries, gooseberries, currants, blackcaps, honey, jams and cut flowers. Seasonal, call for hours: 715-594-3648.

Maiden Rock, Wisconsin

Maiden Rock is 15 miles southeast of Red Wing, MN on Hwy 35.

Maiden Rock's name originates from the legend of a beautiful Dakota girl who chose to leap to her death rather than marry a man she didn't love. The famed rock is less than 5 miles south of town. A historic marker gives the details.

Basil's, Hwy 35, Maiden Rock (located in the charming mid-19th century church). Open Mar–Dec, W–Su. 751-448-3039. Antiques and gift shop.

> **Option:** Look for the **Smiling Pelican Bakery** on Hwy 35 in a cozy 1870s two-story house. Owner Sandra Theilman's culinary works of art are melt-in-your-mouth delicious. Pies, tarts, quiches, scones, muffins, cookies, breads and more. Even treats for your doggie! Open F–Su. 715-448-3807

Stockholm, Wisconsin

Stockholm is 21 miles southeast of Red Wing, MN on Hwy 35. (90-minute drive from the Twin Cities); www.mississippi-river.org/stockholm.html

You'll lose your heart to this Swedish "Eden"—the tiny town (only 89 folks) with the great gardens.

Green Gables, N2037 Spring St (Merchants Hotel building). Open Mar–Dec. Open daily May–Oct. 715-442-2113 or 715-448-2508. Full house of antiques, collectibles, furniture and home accents.

Crocus Oak Co., 111 Spring St. Open mid-Mar–Nov, Th–Su. 715-442-4401. Wide collection of gifts, antiques, furniture and art for the "procurer of good stuff."

> **Options: Stockholm Gardens**, Hwy 35 (east end of town); 715-442-3200. Gorgeous display gardens specializing in wildflowers and the unusual. Their hibiscus have dinner plate-sized blooms. Look for the white picket fence. Open daily May–Oct. Call for hours.

Pepin, Wisconsin

Pepin is 28 miles southeast of Red Wing, MN on Hwy 35.

Pepin is the birthplace of famous children's author Laura Ingalls Wilder. Visitors from around the world sign the guest book noting their pleasure at picnicking on the actual site of Laura's early childhood days.

Lakeview Art/Antiques, 912 1st St (on the lake several blocks west of marina). 715-442-9000 Glassware, some furniture, yard finds.

Wag'n Wheel, N1135 County Rd N; 1 mile on Co N off Hwy 35. Call for hours. 715-442-6292. Barn full of antiques and collectibles.

Alma, Wisconsin

Alma is 44 miles southeast of Red Wing, MN on Hwy 35. (2-hour drive from the Twin Cities); www.almawisconsin.com

Historic Alma is only two blocks wide, but seven miles long. Houses seem as if they're carved from the river bluffs.

Lone Pine Antiques, S1401 Spring Creek Rd. 608-685-4839. Turn off of Hwy 35 north of Alma (by the school) onto Spring Creek Road; follow for two miles winding your way through a picturesque Wisconsin valley. The drive alone is worth taking. Open daily year-round. A barn and five sheds crammed with glassware, primitives, furniture and yard finds.

Options: Rieck's Lake Park is the perfect spot for some serious eagle watching. Nesting season is mid-Mar–mid-Jul. Migrating tundra swans find Rieck's Lake a handy pit stop late Oct–early Nov. Free year-round viewing scope and eagle information. Volunteers on hand to answer questions during swan migrating season. Wheelchair accessible observation deck. Park facilities and campground. Rieck's Lake Park is north of Alma on Hwy 35. 608-685-3330 • **Buena Vista Park** is 500' straight above the Mississippi River. Panoramic view of Alma and the river valley. Awesome sight for those who love heights. Follow sign from Hwy 35. Park facilities. Free. • **Fire & Ice**, 305 N Main St, Alma. The 1868 building is loaded with charm and good things to eat—hand-dipped ice cream cones, gourmet coffees and desserts. Order a bowl of sinfully delicious blueberry cheesecake ice cream and head out back to an amazing "secret garden." The gorgeous Italianate formal garden, carved into the hillside, features fountains, bronze statues and a lovely break from the fast track. Open Memorial Day–Oct.

Wabasha

29 miles south of Red Wing, MN on Hwy 61; www.wabashamn.org or 651-565-4158. From Fountain City, drive north on Hwy 35 to Nelson—bridge crosses the Mississippi River into Wabasha.

More than a town of *Grumpy Old Men*, Wabasha has the largest wintering concentrations of Bald Eagles in the lower 48 states. Established in the 1830s, Wabasha is Minnesota's oldest town.

Wabasha Flea Market, 200 Industrial Ct; off Hwy 61 across from Wabasha. Watch for signs. Sa & Su. 651-565-4767.

> **Options: Anderson House**, 333 W Main St. The Anderson House is Minnesota's oldest operating hotel. Antique-filled rooms, shared and private baths, whirlpool suites and a tabby cat (if you request) curled at your feet for the night—$$–$$$. The Anderson House is also a restaurant known for their breads and desserts. Grandma's sour cream raisin pie never tasted so good—$–$$. Call for hours: 651-565-2500. www.historicandersonhouse.com • **Bridgewaters Bed & Breakfast**. 651-565-4208 or 888-565-4201. www.bridgewatersbandb.com. Six rooms (2 share bath), river view, gardens, full candlelight breakfast—crunchy caramel French toast is a much requested favorite.—$$–$$$. • **Great River Houseboats**, 1009 E Main. 651-565-3376. Looking for something really different in lodging? Look no further than Wabasha Marina Boatyard. Fleet of seven houseboats, each with kitchen and bathroom with shower, sleep up to ten people each. www.greatriverhouseboats.com

Frontenac

Frontenac is north of Lake City on Hwy 61.

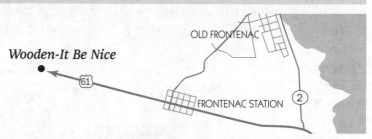

Wooden-It Be Nice, a few miles north of Frontenac on Hwy 61. Open daily. 651-388-7699. Gift shop and antiques, restoration business.

NOTE: Red Wing is less than 8 miles farther north on Hwy 61.

> **Options: Villa Maria Center**, 29847 Co 2 Blvd. 651-345-4582. Originally a convent school for girls, the Villa Maria is now a conference/retreat center. A "prayer trail" leads through the surrounding woods. Visitors welcome daily. Call for hours. • **Old Frontenac Historic District**. Continue on the road past the Villa Maria Center into Old Frontenac, a mid 19th-century look at Minnesota's past. One lane gravel paths overlook Lake Pepin with block after block of restored, Civil War-era two-story homes, white painted clapboards, green shutters and expansive lawns.

NOTE: If you happen to be in the area during the first weekend in May, you're in for tons of deals, steals and squeals as the entire loop (excluding Fountain City) turns into one giant **100-Mile Garage Sale**. Annual event, from dawn to dusk.

NE Bluff Country Antiquing

Antiquing the bluff country is unlike any other experience: quaint small towns, rolling wooded hills and valleys. Any time of year is the perfect time to antique and sightsee.

Winona

120 miles south of the Twin Cities on Hwy 61. Winona Chamber of Commerce, 67 Main St, 507-452-2272; www.visitwinona.com

Built on a sandbar created by the Mississippi River, Winona calls herself the "Island City." From the vantage of the **Garvin Heights** overlook, it's easy to see why. Travel the 2 miles straight up and have a look for yourself. To get to Garvin Heights, turn south off of Hwy 61 on Huff St (opposite direction of Winona) and follow Garvin Heights Road to overlook.

1. **Country Comfort Antique Center**, corner of 3rd & Main. 507-452-7044. Exquisite selection of Victorian furniture and more. Open daily.

2. **A-Z Collectibles**, 152 Main St. 507-454-0366. Closed Saturdays. Other days open by chance or appt.

   Option: Don't miss the gorgeous rose gardens in **Lake Park** located along the riverfront. Band shell, Veterans Memorial, a paved bike and walking trail, paddle boating and canoeing. Take Huff St to Lake Park Dr. • **Pickwick Mill**, take Hwy 61 south to Co 7 (between Winona and La Crescent). 507-457-0499 or 507-452-9658; www.pickwickmill.org. Charming six-story 1858 limestone mill, waterfall and millpond. Open Jun–Aug, Tu–Su. Weekends only in spring and fall. Fee charged.

La Crescent

From Winona, continue south on Hwy 61 where the road joins with I-90. Continue south another 7 miles, watch for signs.

Called the "Apple Capital of Minnesota," La Crescent has the Mississippi River on one side, and apple orchard covered bluffs on the other.

Apple Valley Gifts & Antiques , 329 Main St. 507-895-4268. Lace curtains, country linens, pottery, antiques and more. Open daily.

Houston

Houston is approximately 15 miles southwest of La Crescent on Hwy 16.

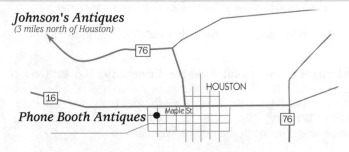

It's easy to understand why they call this region "Bluff Country." Breathtaking scenery, rolling hills and bluffs, hardwood forests and winding roads. Southeastern Minnesota is the only portion of the state that wasn't leveled by glaciers during the Ice Age.

Phone Booth Antiques, 413 W Maple St (1 blk south of Hwy 16, watch for the phone booth!). 507-896-2280. Open year-round. Depression glass and lots of fun '50s stuff. "If you like to bargain, you'll love us!" claims their ad.

Johnson's Antiques, 16946 Todd Dr; 3 miles north of Houston on Hwy 76. Turn right on Doblar Road, first place on left. 507-896-2291. Primitives, general line. Open by chance or appt.

Lanesboro

Lanesboro is southwest of Houston on Hwy 16. Lanesboro Area Chamber of Commerce; 800-944-2670 or 507-467-2696; www.lanesboro.com

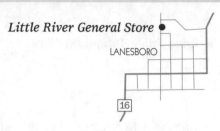

Lanesboro is a treasure trove of history. Nearly the entire downtown district is on the National Register of Historic Places. Flower-lined streets loaded with unique gift shops and restaurants, an old-fashioned ice cream parlor, wineries, Root River State Trail, B&Bs and antiques. The first of Buffalo Bill's Wild West Shows was performed in Lanesboro.

Little River General Store, 105 Coffee St, downtown. 507-467-2943 or 800-994-2943. Open M–Su. Toy tractor memorabilia, beer collectibles, lanterns and lamps, general line. www.lrgeneralstore.net.

NOTE: Little River General Store also rents bikes, canoes and cross-country skis.

> **Options: Commonweal Theatre Company**, 206 Parkway N 800-657-7025 or 507-467-2525. www.commonwealtheatre.org. Experience live, professional theater Feb–Dec. Call for performance schedule. • **Scenic Valley Winery**, 101 Coffee St. 507-467-2958. Open daily, Apr–Dec. Sample local wines in the downtown sales room.

Preston

Preston is southwest of Lanesboro on Hwy 16.

Preston is the Fillmore County seat.

The Red Bench, 132 St. Anthony St S (on the Courthouse Square). 507-765-2731. Open W–Sa. Glass, sports memorabilia, advertising and interesting stuff.

> **Options:** A stay at Preston's jail would be quite a treat, as long as it's the 1869 **Jail House Historic Inn**, 109 Houston St. 507-765-2181; www.jailhouseinn.com. Twelve rooms with private baths, fireplaces, whirlpools, a 2-story porch, full breakfast. The Cell Block suite retains some of its "original" decor. • **Historic Forestville** is roughly 7 miles west of Preston off of Hwy 12. Tour the 1890s town complete with costumed interpreters. State Park permit required. NOTE: See the Mystery Cave Tour (p. 98) for more details. • The town of **Fountain** is the self-proclaimed "sinkhole capitol of the U.S." Located 4 miles north of Preston on Hwy 52, have a look at one of the sinkholes at a wayside stop.

Chatfield

Chatfield is less than 15 miles north of Preston on Hwy 52.

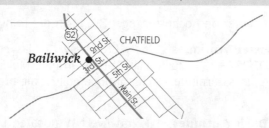

Frequently referred to as the "Chosen Valley," Chatfield is home to the International Band Music Lending Library and Pease Wildlife Museum. Several miles west on Co 101 is an old stone house where the Jesse James gang once stayed.

Bailiwick, 204 S Main St. 507-867-3076. Open M–Sa. General line of antiques and collectibles plus gifts.

Stewartville

Stewartville is west of Chatfield on Hwy 30.

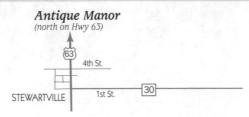

Antique Manor
(north on Hwy 63)

The people of Stewartville welcome visitors to come and see what it's like to live a "wonderful life." Small town atmosphere with plenty of friendly folks.

Antique Manor, 1600 2nd Ave NW (on Hwy 63—only 7 miles south of Rochester). 507-533-9300. Open M–Sa. Full line. Multi-dealer shop.

Rochester

Rochester is 7 miles north of Stewartville on Hwy 63; 507-288-4331; www.rochestercvb.org or www.visitrochestermn.com

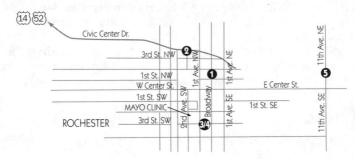

NOTE: See chapter on Rochester (pg. 120) for more things to do.

1. **Old Rooster Antiques**, 106 N Broadway (3 blks north of Radisson Hotel). 507-287-6228. Open daily. Parking in rear. Multi-dealers featuring stoneware, toys, furniture, clocks, antique doll repair, brass hardware and more.

2. **Churn Dash Antiques**, 411 2nd Ave NW (located in Collins Feed & Seed, 2 blks north of Methodist Hospital). 507-289-4844. Open M–Sa. Furniture, glassware, primitives, toys, kitchen collectibles and more.

3. **Antique Mall On Third St**, 18 3rd St SW (lower level). 507-287-0684. Open daily.

4. **John Kruesel's General Merchandise**, 22 3rd St SW. 507-289-8049 Open Tu–Sa. American antiques, early lighting, jewelry, consulting, restoration. www.kruesel.com.

5. **Peterson's Antiques & Stripping**, 111 11th Ave NE (11 blks from downtown). 507-282-9100 or 507-289-0277. Open M–Sa by chance or appt. Specializing in antique furniture, refinished or as-is. Furniture restoration.

NOTE: You have a choice to make. You can either continue north on Hwy 52 into the Twin Cities, or take Hwy 14 east to Winona.

Highway 52 Route North—Oronoco

From Rochester, take Hwy 52 north toward the Twin Cities.

This small town of Oronoco (off of Hwy 52) plays host to the annual Gold Rush Days. On the third weekend in August, thousands of folks converge for the huge flea market.

1. **Antiques Oronoco**, on Hwy 52. 507-367-2220. Open W–Su. Huge showroom, old book area & barn with rough items. www.antiques-oronoco.com

2. **Berg's Antique Store**, 50/420 Minnesota Ave S. 507-367-4413 or 507-367-4588. Open Apr–Dec, Tu–Sa. In business since 1963. Advertising, furniture, toys.

3. **Mom's Antique Mall**, 1110 Minnesota Ave S. 507-367-2600. Over 30 dealers.

Pine Island

Pine Island is north of Oronoco on Hwy 52.

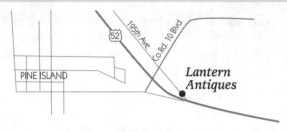

Lantern Antiques, 1100 E Frontage Rd (red brick house on Hwy 52). 507-356-4215. Log cabin and summer kitchen full of refinished, painted and "as found" furniture, primitives and accessories. Closed Jan & Feb. Open weekends by chance or appt.

Cannon Falls

Cannon Falls is north of Pine Island on Hwy 52.

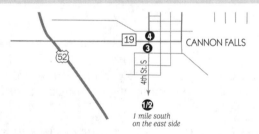

1. **Country Side Antique Mall**, 31752 65th Ave. (on the right as you come into town from the south—next to the John Deere dealership). 507-263-0352; www.csamantiques.com. Open daily. Over 40 dealers. Large selection of antiques, collectibles and furniture.

2. **Thora Mae's Antique Mall**, 31265 County Blvd, located in the mall. 507-263-2073. Open daily. 60 dealers.

3. **Fourth Street Antiques**, 106 S 4th St (half blk south of Hwy 19 on 4th St) 507-263-7249. Call for hours. 12-dealer shop.

4. **Schaffer's Antiques**, 111 N 4th St (downtown). 507-263-5200. Call for hours. General line, furniture, primitives, tools, pottery, pictures and stoneware.

Option: Cannon River Winery, 421 Mill Street W (downtown), Cannon Falls; 507-263-7400; www.cannonriverwinery.com If you spot a gorgeous vintage brick building with massive red double doors, you've found the charming Cannon River Winery. The winery features about eighteen hand-crafted vintages including a nice apple wine and free tastings during business hours. Call for guided tours of the facility and vineyard. Their website posts bottling dates and times. Seasonal hours.

Highway 14 Route West—Eyota

Eyota, if you wish to return to Winona, from Rochester drive west 12 miles on Hwy 14.

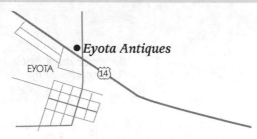

Eyota Antiques, 30 S Front St SW; Hwy 14. 507-545-1958. Open Apr–Nov, Sa & Su. Many toys, fat tire bikes, fishing collectibles and more.

St. Charles

St. Charles is west of Eyota on Hwy 14. St. Charles City Hall; 507-932-3020.

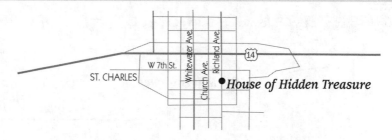

House of Hidden Treasure (1859), 807 Richland Ave. 507-932-3577. Open Apr–Dec, daily. Twelve rooms, a garage and a barn full, too. General line. Advertised as "a place where you can dig and lots of dust."

SW Bluff Country Antiquing

Not much beats a trip into the beautiful bluff country, unless, of course, it's a trip into the bluff country to hunt antiques.

Spring Grove

From the Twin Cities, take Hwy 61 south until it turns into I-90 (beyond Winona). Follow I-90 south to Hwy 44. Drive southwest on Hwy 44 to Spring Grove.

Spring Grove is Minnesota's first Norwegian settlement. Check out their mile-high meringue pie, ten flavors of Spring Grove pop, the Trinity Church carillon and window boxes with rosemaling.

Ballard House Antiques & Specialty Shop, 163 W Main. 507-498-5434. Seasonal, call for hours.

Mabel

Mabel is approximately 8 miles west of Spring Grove on Hwy 44.

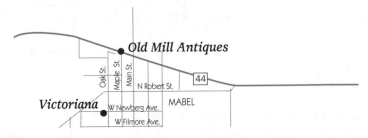

Charles Lindbergh, in his barnstorming days, visited Mabel and gave many of the residents airplane rides. Mabel's Steam Engine Museum displays large steamers, gas engines and threshers.

Victoriana, 316 W Newburg Ave. 507-493-5696. Call for hours or appt. Three floors of Victorian furniture, Oriental rugs and accessories.

Old Mill Antiques, 416 N Maple St; Jct. Hwy 44 & Maple St. 507-493-

5000 or 507-493-5025. Call for hours. Full line of antiques, dried flowers, furniture, glassware, primitives, stoneware, Americana and more.

Harmony

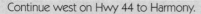

Continue west on Hwy 44 to Harmony.

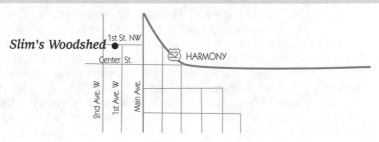

Guided Amish tours and cave explorations are a couple of good reasons to visit Harmony. Another is for their antiques!

Slim's Woodshed, 160 1st St NW; www.slimswoodshed.com; 507-886-3114. Call for hours. You can do it all at Slim's: shop for antiques, take lessons in wood carving and tour the wood carving museum—home of the Caricature Carvers of America Circus. Fee charged for a 1-hour guided tour of museum; free for ages 5 and under.

Austin

From Harmony, follow Hwy 52 north to Hwy 16 west to I-90W; follow I-90W into town.

Where does Spam™ come from? Hormel, of course. Austin is their company headquarters.

Twice As Nice Antiques & Collectibles, 417 N Main St. 507-433-5353. Open year-round, M–F. General line plus furniture.

NOTE: Hwy 56 is also the **Shooting Star Scenic Byway**. The 32-mile, state designated wildflower route is the only place in Minnesota you'll find a wild primrose called the shooting star.

> **Option:** Tour the **Spam™ Museum**, 1937 Spam Blvd. 800-LUV-SPAM (800-588-7726) or 507-437-5100. www.spam.com/museum. Interactive displays, games and puppet show within 16,500 square feet. Open daily. Free admission and gifts. • **J.C. Hormel Nature Center**, 1304 21st St NE; 507-437-7519. Once part of the former Hormel estate, explore this beautiful nature center that includes an interpretive building, hiking through woods, gardens, orchards, a pond and streams. Canoe in the summer and cross-country ski in the winter (rentals available for a small fee). Wheelchair accessible trails. Open daily, year-round; free. Visitor center closed on Sundays. • **Mower County Historical Society**, Mower County Fairgrounds, 1303 6th Ave SW; 507-437-6082. More than twenty buildings house the history of Austin and Mower County. See a steam locomotive, horse-drawn carriages, authentic Native American tools and clothing, vintage firefighting equipment, miniature handmade three-ring circus and much more. Open Tu–Fri year-round. Small fee charged. • **The Old Mill Restaurant**, 54446 244th St; 507-437-2076, www.oldmill.net. Built in 1872, the restaurant (once a busy flour mill) overlooks the scenic Cedar River. They offer a full dinner menu, an extensive wine and beer selection, and a long list of to-die-for desserts. Reservations appreciated.

Kasson

Take Co 13 north.

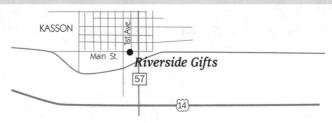

Miller's Antiques & Used Merchandise, 110 W Main. 507-634-6531. Open daily. Buys complete households.

Mantorville

3 miles north of Kasson on Hwy 57.

Riverside Gifts, 521 N Main. 507-635-5464. Call for hours. Antiques, collectibles, candles, Amish furniture and more.

Memorabilia Antiques, next to Opera House. 507-635-5419. Call for days and hours. General line of antiques, glassware, china, pottery, furniture.

NOTE: See pg. 124 of the Rochester chapter for more about Mantorville.

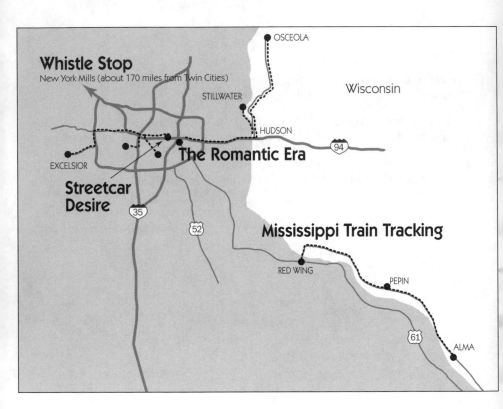

Whistle Stop
New York Mills (about 170 miles from Twin Cities)

OSCEOLA

Wisconsin

STILLWATER

HUDSON

94

EXCELSIOR

The Romantic Era

Streetcar Desire

35

52

Mississippi Train Tracking

RED WING

PEPIN

61

ALMA

THEME: *TRAINS, TRAINS & MORE TRAINS*

Whistle Stop

Streetcar Desire

The Romantic Era

Mississippi Train Tracking

*I*f you love everything about trains, from their screaming whistles to their clacking wheels, then this chapter is for you. Enjoy all the train rides, museums, depots, toys, restaurants and streetcars in the pages ahead, but save some time for exploring the many interesting area attractions included in the options.

TRAINS

Whistle Stop

New York Mills is 30 miles SE of Detroit Lakes on Hwy 10 between Perham and Wadena.

Whistle Stop Inn Bed & Breakfast

New York Mills, 1 blk south, then 1 blk east of 4-way stop; 800-328-6315 or 218-385-2223; www.whistlestopbedandbreakfast.com

Whistle Stop Inn Bed & Breakfast

All aboard! This is one of the quietest train trips you'll ever take, because not one of the five railroad cars ever goes anywhere. Whistle Stop innkeepers Jann and Roger Lee offer a truly unique experience: plush overnight accommodations in elegant vintage railroad cars. Two cars feature double whirlpools, fireplace and sitting rooms; another showcases an antique claw-foot tub. All include in-room coffee and tea service and full breakfast. Open year-round.—$$–$$$.

Accommodations at the Whistle Stop Inn are also available in the gorgeous 1903 Victorian home. Oak woodwork, antiques, railroad memorabilia.

NOTE: New York Mills, a town of 1,000, was named one of the top five culturally cool towns by *USA Today Weekend Magazine*. Located about 170 miles from the Twin Cities, it's only one hour away from Itasca State Park. See the Harley Trip in the Extreme Adventures chapter on pg. 44 for more things to do.

> **Options: New York Mills Regional Cultural Center**, 24 N Main Ave. 218-385-3339. www.kulcher.org. The center features musical performances, gallery exhibits, summer art classes and the annual **Great American Think-Off**. Hosted on the Sunday before Father's Day, the Think-Off draws essay contestants from around the world, ranging from a 15-year-old cheerleader to a priest from New York. An on-line C-SPAN audience, as well as the theater audience, vote on the winner. A past debate topic posed: The Nature of Humanity: Inherently Good or Inherently Evil? Oddly enough, the debate ended in a tie—the only one in the Think-Off's ten-year history. • See the **World's Largest Art Tractor** in Sculpture Park,

New York Mills. • **Finn Creek Open Air Museum**, 218-385-2233. Tour the restored 18-acre farm established in 1900 by Finnish immigrants Siffert and Wilhelmina Tapio. Original house and sauna, blacksmith shop and barns. Open Memorial Day–Labor Day, daily. Located 3 miles east of New York Mills on Hwy 10, south 2.5 miles on Hwy 106, then a half mile west on a gravel road.

Streetcar Desire

This fun day begins in St. Paul for a tour of the state's first locomotive repair shop and ends with a ride on one of the oldest operating museum-quality trolleys in the country.

Jackson Street Roundhouse

193 E Pennsylvania Ave, St. Paul; 651-228-0263. (Take Pennsylvania Ave exit off I-35E and go 2 blks west.); www.mtmuseum.org

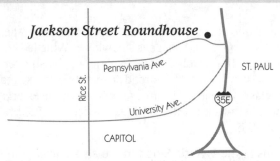

Built in 1862 by the Minnesota and Pacific Railroad, the Jackson Street Roundhouse stands on the site of Minnesota's first locomotive repair shop. James J. Hill, founder of the Great Northern Railway, rebuilt the structure to its present form. The Jackson Street Roundhouse closed in 1960.

The grounds feature historical railroad equipment and an interpretive center. Fascinating exhibits bring alive the sights and sounds of the golden railroad era. Open year-round. Wheelchair accessible. Fee charged.

Minnehaha Depot

4926 Minnehaha Ave in Minnehaha Park, Minneapolis; 651-228-0263. (Take Hiawatha Ave. [Hwy 55] to E 46th St, turn east. Turn right on 46th Ave S; right on Godfrey Pkwy; park on the left.); www.mtmuseum.org

Delicate gingerbread architecture earned the Minnehaha Depot a title of "Princess." The 1875 depot served as a freight station until 1963 and is now owned by the Minnesota Historical Society. Step inside and listen to train sounds from the 1920s or operate the telegraph key. Open Memorial Day–Labor Day on Sundays. Free.

Como-Harriet Streetcar Line

Board streetcars at the Linden Hills Station, Queen Ave S and W 42nd St, on the west shore of Lake Harriet, Minneapolis. (From I-35W, exit at 46th St, follow 46th St west to Lake Harriet Pkwy, and follow Pkwy past the band shell to W 42nd St); 952-922-1096 or www.trolleyride.com

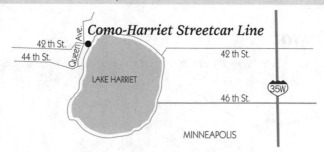

Enjoy a trip back to the 1900s aboard the antique, century-old streetcars. A 2-mile, 15-minute ride costs $2.00 and is worth every cent. Visit the station exhibits and museum store or take a leisurely walk around the lake. Memorial Day–Labor Day, M–F: 6:30 p.m. to dusk, Sa & Su: 12:30 p.m. to dusk. Sep & Oct: weekends only.

Excelsior Streetcar Line

From Minneapolis, take Hwy 7 to the Excelsior exit to Water St. The platform is on the left. 952-922-1096 or www.trolleyride.com

Take a one-mile ride on Car No. 78. The beautifully restored yellow streetcar is one of the oldest operating museum-quality trolleys in the country. Catch the streetcar May–Oct. Fee charged, free for children 3 and under.

NOTE: For more ideas on what to do while in Excelsior, see the section in the Romantic Getaways chapter on pg. 134.

The Romantic Era

These attractions are for romantics and train lovers alike. Begin in St. Paul with lunch at the Union Depot, then take an hour-long scenic drive northeast into Wisconsin. Board a vintage train in Osceola for a leisurely ride, then end your day in historic Stillwater for an elegant five-course dinner aboard the Minnesota Zephyr.

Union Depot

214 E 4th St, downtown St. Paul (from Warner Rd heading southwest, turn right on Sibley).

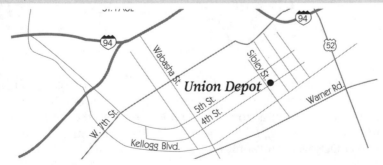

This once bustling 1917 train station is now home to some of St. Paul's finest restaurants. Elegant interior of massive marble pillars, granite floors

and beautiful ironwork. Live entertainment on the weekends. Choice of foods range from Greek to barbecue and everything in between. Lunch begins around 11 a.m., noon on weekends.—$.

NOTE: Most restaurants also offer dinner.

Historic 1916 Osceola Depot

114 Depot Rd, Osceola, WI; 715-755-3570 or 651-228-0263; www.trainride.org

Historic 1916 Osceola Depot

Begin your vintage rail experience with the purchase of a ticket at the fully restored 1916 SOO Line Depot. Constructed of wire-cut red brick and white sandstone, the depot was a marvel in its day, featuring both mens' and ladies' indoor toilets.

The Osceola & St. Croix Valley Railroad offers round trips aboard diesel powered trains. The westbound 90-minute trip traverses steep rock cliffs and an untamed river valley, while the shorter, 50-minute eastbound trip passes through miles of picturesque Wisconsin dairyland. Special scheduled trips include Caboose Rides, Fireworks Express, William O'Brien Naturalist Trip, Fall Leaf Watchers Trip and more (some include meals). Call or check website for dates and ticket prices. Gift shop in depot; store on the train. Mid-Apr through Oct: Sat, Su & holidays. Fee charged.

Options: Loaded with Midwestern friendliness and old-fashioned charm, there's more to do in Osceola than ride trains. Stretch the legs with a hike down a winding stairway (131 steps) to beautiful **Cascade Falls**, conveniently located on Cascade Street, Osceola's main drag. • Enjoy a fantastic view of the falls in the Secret Garden behind the **Coffee Connection**, 99 Cascade St N. 715-755-3833. This homey restaurant serves up tasty muffins, sandwiches and pies.—$. Grab a cup of coffee and relax on a bench in the garden or challenge someone to a game of checkers—adult and child versions on hand.

Minnesota Zephyr

601 N Main, Stillwater; 800-992-6100 then press 1 or 651-430-3000; www.minnesotazephyr.com

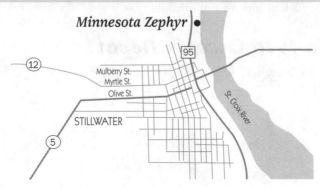

Journey back in time to the late 1940s on the elegant, carefully restored Minnesota Zephyr. Each of the five dining cars is different in design and color, recreating prestigious railroad dining of bygone days. The 3-hour excursion along the river and woodland bluffs includes a 5-course white linen dinner and features the Zephyr Cabaret performing the hits of the '40s and '50s. Open year-round. $$$$ + $. Free entrance to depot and museum.

Mississippi Train Tracking

These attractions follow the rail tracks along the Mississippi River from Red Wing, MN to Alma, WI. From the Twin Cities, take Hwy 61 south to Red Wing (about 50 miles).

Caribou Coffee

726 Main St, Red Wing, MN. 651-388-1910; www.cariboucoffee.com

For anyone into trains, this is one coffee house you're going to want to see.

Built at the turn of the twentieth century, there's a real sense of déja vu as you stand in line to place an order. It's not hard to imagine a bustling depot of travelers standing in line to purchase tickets. The two-story red brick building has customer seating on both levels. Wheelchair accessible—$.

Red Wing Visitors and Convention Bureau

420 Levee St (behind the St. James Hotel); 800-498-3444 or 651-385-5934; www.redwing.org

Located in the Amtrak and Greyhound Depot (building listed on the National Register of Historic Places), the friendly staff at the Red Wing Visitors and Convention Bureau can hook you up with anything from fishing guides to upcoming city events. Check out all their wonderful train memorabilia. Open M–F.

Levee Park

Bush and Levee Sts (behind St. James Hotel), Red Wing, MN

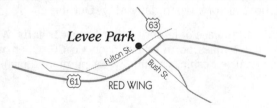

The Levee Park vantage offers front row viewing of the Continental Grain Company's cargo train loading operation.

Options: Although this has nothing to do with trains, follow Levee St west to **Bay Point Park**. Marvel at the skill required of tug captains as they maneuver barges through one of the sharpest turns on the Mississippi River. The park is also home to the **Boathouse Village**, a rare remaining example of a "gin pole" system. The system allows boathouses to adjust to the different water levels by riding up and down on poles. • Get a sweeping view of Red Wing from **Memorial Park**; especially breathtaking during the fall "leaf season." Take E 7th St to Skyline Dr • **Barn Bluff** is a favorite spot for hikers and cliff climbers. There are two trails leading to the top: the front trail with concrete steps and the more difficult river-side hike through the woods. Take E 5th St pass under Hwy 61. Trail begins on left side. Free. • **Red Wing Riverboat Rides**, owned and operated by Bob Schleichen. 651-388-3047. Board Captain Bob's pride, *Maggie*, for an hour-long excursion on the Mississippi. Grab your birding binoculars. Soda pop available. Daily May–Oct. Departure from Levee Wall (behind St. James Hotel). Call for appointment. Fee charged. • **Falconer Vineyards**, 3572 Old Tyler Rd. 651-388-8849, www.FalconerVineyards.com. Open weekends May–Nov. You'll enjoy the beautiful river valley scenery as well as the wines. Pack a picnic basket and soak in the view. Small fee charged for wine sampling.

Pepin Railroad Depot Museum

Pepin, WI. Pepin Park on Hwy 35 (28 miles from Red Wing, MN). From Red Wing, take Hwy 63 across the Mississippi River, then turn right (east) on Hwy 35. 715-442-6501

Stepping into this 110-year-old railroad station is a walk back through time. Manned with knowledgeable volunteers, the building is jam-packed with railroad and riverboat history. Open daily May–Oct. Free.

Option: Visit the birthplace of famed author **Laura Ingalls Wilder**. The wayside is located 7 miles north of Pepin on Co CC. Open year-round. Includes a reconstructed cabin, working water pump and picnic facilities. Free.

Lock and Dam No. 4

Alma, WI. Observation deck on Hwy 35 (16 miles from Pepin).

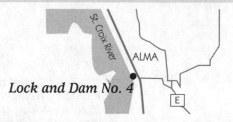

Lock and Dam No. 4

You're probably wondering what a lock and dam is doing on a train tour. To get to the observation deck, you first have to cross the train tracks—accomplished via an open catwalk. Stop midway on the catwalk while a train rushes directly below your feet. There's nothing quite as exhilarating (or terrifying!) as experiencing these mighty beasts from point-blank range. You won't have to wait long for a train, as more than 50 pass this spot daily. Free.

> **Option:** While in Alma, venture 500' uphill to **Buena Vista Park**. *Better Homes and Gardens* magazine referred to the view as "one of the river valley's finest natural balconies." Take Hwy E and follow signs; 2½ miles. Open year-round. Picnic tables, scenic overlook, hiking trail. Free.

NOTE: For more about Alma, see pg. 151.

Grand Portage State Park
Judge C.R. Magney State Park
Cascade River State Park
Temperance River State Park
Tettegouche State Park

GRAND MARAIS

Gooseberry Falls State Park

Lake Superior

North Shore Scenic Drive

DULUTH

Amnicon & Pattison State Parks

Amnicon Falls State Park

Pattison State Park

35

Wisconsin

Follow the Falls

Saint Anthony Falls
Historic District
Minnehaha Falls

Vermillion Falls

Cannon Falls

Zumbrota

ROCHESTER

WINONA

52

THEME: Waterfalls

North Shore Scenic Drive

Amnicon & Pattison State Parks

Follow the Falls

*I*f you're crazy about waterfalls, this chapter will put you over the edge. The North Shore Scenic Drive alone includes more than 20 falls, and that's not counting the ones tumbling from the rocks along the highway!

North Shore Scenic Drive

From Duluth, head north on Scenic Hwy 61 to the Canadian border (about 150 miles).

Each year, the North Shore Scenic Drive—Minnesota's most romantic tour of the Lake Superior shoreline—draws visitors by the millions. One trip around this block and you'll know why.

NOTE: Minnesota state parks require vehicle permits. Information about purchasing permits is available at the DNR website: www.dnr.state.mn.us/state_parks/permit.html

> **Option:** Lake Superior, the largest of the five Great Lakes, holds ten percent of the world's fresh water—the average temperature is 40°F. It is breathtaking and deadly, having claimed hundreds of ships over the years. A good place to start any exploration of the North Shore is the **Lake Superior Maritime Visitor Center**. It provides a history of the lake and features full-sized replicas of ship cabins, an operating steam engine, film presentations and more. Located on the waterfront in Canal Park next to the Aerial Lift Bridge. 218-720-5260 ext 1; or www.lsmma.com. Open year-round. Wheelchair accessible. Free.

Gooseberry Falls State Park

> 3206 Hwy 61, Two Harbors; 218-834-3855;
> www.dnr.state.mn.us/state_parks/gooseberry_falls/index.html

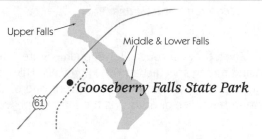

Gooseberry Falls State Park receives nearly a million visitors annually. It features 5 waterfalls with 18 miles of picturesque hiking trails. The interior trails cross the Gooseberry River several times via foot bridges. The visitor center includes a rest stop, a nature store, an interpretive center and maps of the trails. Open year-round. Those who use the park as a rest stop need not buy a permit. Wheelchair accessible.

> **Options:** Although you won't see any waterfalls, a stop at **Split Rock Lighthouse** is a must. Built in 1910, the lighthouse commands a magnificent view of Lake Superior from atop a 130' cliff. Tour of the lighthouse,

fog-signal building and keeper's home conducted daily mid-May through mid-Oct. The history center is open Sa–Su during some winter months. www.mnhs.org/places/sites/srl or 218-226-6372. Gift shop, interactive history center, movie. Fee charged. • Take a guided tour of **Minnesota's only operating light station** (also a B&B!) 1 Lighthouse Point, Two Harbors. 888-832-5606. (About 30 miles north of Duluth on Hwy 61). Fee charged. • Built in 1898, tour Minnesota Mining and Manufacturing's (3M's) first office building, now the only **sandpaper museum** in the world. Hands-on interactive programs. 2nd Ave and Waterfront Dr, Two Harbors. Lake County Historical Society. 888-573-5701. www.twoharborsmn.com. Fee charged. • Hwy 61 offers many access points for the **Superior Hiking Trail**, named one of the world's top 25 trails. Two hundred miles of rugged and challenging territory. 218-834-2700. www.shta.org.

Tettegouche State Park

5702 Hwy 61, Silver Bay; 218-226-6365;
www.dnr.state.mn.us/state_parks/tettegouche/index.html

The Baptism River flows through Tettegouche State Park creating three waterfalls, including the spectacular 60' High Falls. Hike to the historic logging camp on Mic Mac Lake, or better still, rent one of the no frills rustic cabins. Twenty-three miles of trails. Visitor center with exhibits open year-round.

Options: Get a sweeping view of Lake Superior from the 350' high **Palisade Head**. Cliffs have colorful red outcrops. Overlook is on the right side of Hwy 61, directly before Tettegouche State Park entrance. Watch for sign. • **Northshore Mining** offers free 90-minute tours of its taconite plant every Tu, Th and Sa, June–Sept. 10 Outer Drive, Silver Bay. 218-226-4125. • **Caribou Falls Wayside** is 12 miles farther north on the left side of Hwy 61. Stretch the legs with a short, very scenic hike to the falls (less than a mile). Rugged trail. • Continuing north on Hwy 61, view the **Cross River Falls** and gorge from the highway bridge in Schroeder.

Temperance River State Park

7620 Hwy 61 E, PO Box 33, Schroeder; 218-663-7476;
www.dnr.state.mn.us/state_parks/temperance_river/index.html

Within the park, the Temperance River drops 162' in a half-mile series of cascades, creating cauldrons and giant potholes. Hidden Falls is upriver from the parking area along Hwy 61. Over 8 miles of trails. Open year-round.

> **Option: Lutsen Mountains** offers a 2-mile gondola ride with a breathtaking view of Lake Superior and surrounding mountain ridges. Off of Hwy 61, Lutsen. 218-663-7281. www.lutsen.com.

Cascade River State Park

3481 Hwy 61 W, Lutsen; 218-387-3053;
www.dnr.state.mn.us/state_parks/cascade_river/index.html

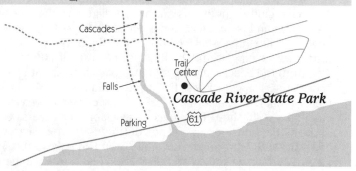

Numerous waterfalls are created by the Cascade River as it twists through a rocky gorge, dropping 225' in one mile. Fifteen miles of gorgeous trails. Open year-round.

> **Option:** The **Gunflint Trail** begins at scenic Grand Marais . Have a pizza topped with wild rice and sauerkraut (or whatever your tastebuds desire) at the famous Sven and Ole's located at 9 W Wisconsin St. Stroll out to the Grand Marais lighthouse and watch the waves crash against the breakers.

Judge C.R. Magney State Park

4051 Hwy 61, Grand Marais; 218-387-3039;
www.dnr.state.mn.us/state_parks/judge_cr_magney/index.html

Set out along the Brule River trail in Judge C.R. Magney State Park to hunt for agates and waterfalls. The Brule divides around a large boulder—one side falls 50' into a pool below, while the other plunges into a pothole known as the Devil's Kettle and is never seen again. Three waterfalls and nine miles of trails.

Option: Built in 1929 along the shoreline of Lake Superior, **Naniboujou Lodge's** original owners intended it as an exclusive club for the wealthy. However, the stock market crash lead to its mortgage foreclosure and sale. After changing many hands and much disrepair, the lodge underwent a restoration and is on the National Register of Historic Places. Retaining its original Cree Indian design, the Naniboujou Great Hall serves as the restaurant's dining room. The fireplace consists of 200 tons of stone gathered from the beach, making it Minnesota's largest native stone fireplace. There are 24 guest rooms: five have wood-burning fireplaces. Delicious meals prepared by gourmet chefs. Afternoon teas served in the solarium/library. Gift shop. Box lunches available for hikers. Open mid-May through Oct. and most weekends during the winter season. Closed Nov and Apr.—$$. 20 Naniboujou Trail, Grand Marais (directly across from Judge C.R. Magney State Park). 218-387-2688. www.naniboujou.com.

Grand Portage State Park

9393 Hwy 61 W, Grand Portage; 218-475-2360;
www.dnr.state.mn.us/state_parks/grand_portage/index.html

About as close to the Canadian border as a Minnesotan can get, Grand Portage State Park features two waterfalls. A half-mile hike leads to the incredible 120' High Falls on the Pigeon River (wheelchair accessible). Another 3.5 mile trail takes you to Middle Falls.

Options: Established in 1731, Grand Portage was Minnesota's first white settlement. Costumed interpreters at the **Grand Portage National Monument** demonstrate birch bark canoe making, adobe oven bread baking and all sorts of other eighteenth century crafts. Off Hwy 61 in Grand Portage. Watch for signs. 218-387-2788. Fee charged. • Spend a day fishing and exploring or camp the weekend on **Isle Royale National Park**. The only way to get there is by boat. Grand Portage Isle Royale Transportation Line, Inc. 888-746-2305 or 715-392-2100; www.grand-isle-royale.com.

Amnicon & Pattison State Parks

Located on the western tip of Wisconsin, Amnicon and Pattison State Parks feature many spectacular waterfalls and they're only a short drive from Duluth. (150 miles from the Twin Cities)

Amnicon Falls State Park

10 miles southeast of Superior, WI on Hwy 2. Follow signs. 715-398-3000

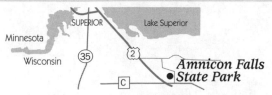

Amnicon Falls State Park has one of the most beautiful series of cascades and waterfalls in the Midwest. At the heart of the park, the Amnicon River separates, forming two streams. Three waterfalls plunge nearly 30' each. During good water flow, the river fills another channel producing a fourth falls. A rare, 55' Horton bowstring bridge spans the river, giving access to an island. Only five other Horton bridges are known to exist. The view of the Lower Falls is wheelchair accessible. Open year-round. Park permit required.

> **Option:** Sorry, no waterfalls at **Wisconsin Point**, just an unforgettably spectacular view of Lake Superior. Miles of sandy beach, lighthouse (not open for tours), Indian cemetery and an excellent place to hunt agates. Located on the outskirts of Superior, Wisconsin. From Superior, take E 2nd St to Moccasin Mike Rd. Turn north onto Wisconsin Point Rd.

Pattison State Park

Located 13 miles south of Superior on Hwy 35, or 20 miles southwest of Amnicon Falls State Park. From Amnicon, retrace your route on Hwy 2 (north toward Superior) to Co Z (west), take Co A south to Co B, follow signs. 715-399-3111

At 165 dizzying feet high, Big Manitou Falls is the highest waterfall in Wisconsin. One mile farther south (on Hwy 35), Little Manitou Falls measures in with a drop of 31'. Pattison State Park is also the site of a 1930s Civilian Conservation Corps camp. Nature center, hiking trails, geology walk, camping, fishing, swimming beach and bath house, picnic facilities. Winter activities include 4½ miles of cross-country ski trails, snowshoeing, hiking and ice skating. Open year-round. Wheelchair accessible. Park permit required.

Follow the Falls

Explore several waterfalls and Minnesota's last remaining covered bridge—all within a comfortable hour's drive of the Twin Cities.

St. Anthony Falls

St. Anthony Falls Historic District, on the Mississippi River between Plymouth Ave N and the 35W bridge in Minneapolis.

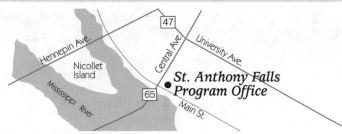

St. Anthony Falls holds the honored distinction of being the only waterfall on the Mississippi River. The falls are only 13', but the actual drop is around 50', making it the longest drop on the river as well.

View the falls from the restored Stone Arch Bridge and explore the 19th century Nicollet Island neighborhood. Tour the industrial ruins of the Minneapolis flour milling district, once the largest in the world. Trail open year-round. Guided walking tours (around 2 miles) offered May–Oct, W–Su. Wheelchair accessible. Fee charged for walking tour.

Program office is at 125 Main St SE (across the river from downtown). Exhibits, movie, information and gift shop. 612-627-5433; www.mnhs.org/places/sites/safhd/index.html

Minnehaha Falls

Inside Minnehaha Park off of Minnehaha Pkwy.

An awesome sight of rushing water over a limestone ledge, but during a

dry season Minnehaha Falls isn't much more than a dribble. A convenient stairway leads to a closer view.

> **Option:** While here, be sure to visit the **Minnehaha Depot**. Operate the telegraph key and listen to train sounds from the 1920s. 651-228-0263. www.mnhs.org/places/sites/md. Open Memorial Day–Labor Day on Sundays. Free.

Vermillion Falls

Hastings, follow Hwy 55, turn south onto Hwy 61, turn left on 21st St E by the Con Agra Flour Mill (immediately after Co 47 junction)

Probably the best kept secret the enchanting river town of Hastings has is the Vermillion Falls. Against a backdrop of old limestone, the 50' wide, 19' high falls makes an ideal place for a picnic. So spread the checkered cloth and pass around the chicken salad while enjoying a picture-perfect view.

NOTE: The mill is the oldest continuing flour milling operation in Minnesota. About a half mile below the falls are the remains of the state's first flour mill, built in 1857. Follow trail.

> **Option: Historic Hastings** has a well preserved downtown district with fine dining, antique shops and specialty stores. For more information, contact the Hastings Area Chamber of Commerce and Tourism Bureau, 111 E 3rd St, Hastings, MN. 888-612-6122 or 651-437-6775. www.hastingsmn.org

Cannon Falls

Cannon Falls, take Hwy 61 south to Co 20. Follow signs.

In actuality, Cannon Falls is a man-made dam, recently reduced to a bump, but still worth the trip. Look for it on the right side as you enter town from the north. Enjoy the park's resident swans and ducks. Stroll the pretty main drag with its quaint gift and antiques shops. Cannon Falls is a real find for those folks needing a relaxing day away from it all.

> **Option:** The 20-mile, paved **Cannon Valley Trail** (former Chicago Great Western Railroad line) runs along the Cannon River from Cannon Falls to Red Wing. Very scenic trail used by hikers, bikers and cross-country skiers.

Zumbrota

Zumbrota is a short 20-mile trip south of Cannon Falls on Hwy 52.

It's not your imagination—the towns really are getting smaller, but ever larger on charm and scenery. Zumbrota is a mix of rolling farmland and river country. No waterfall, but it is the proud home of Minnesota's last remaining covered bridge—and it's painted red too! Located very near its original site, the 1869 bridge was the main stagecoach route between Iowa and St. Paul. Where can you find this magnificent marvel? Where else but in Covered Bridge Park. Look for it on the edge of town heading northeast on Hwy 58.

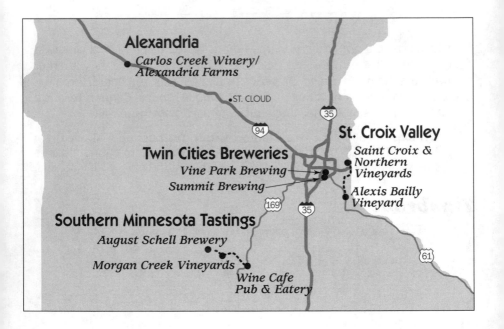

Alexandria
• *Carlos Creek Winery/*
  Alexandria Farms

•ST. CLOUD

35

St. Croix Valley

94

Twin Cities Breweries
Vine Park Brewing
Summit Brewing

Saint Croix &
Northern
Vineyards

Alexis Bailly
Vineyard

169   35

Southern Minnesota Tastings
August Schell Brewery
Morgan Creek Vineyards

Wine Cafe
Pub & Eatery

61

THEME: *WINE & BEER LOVERS' TOURS*

Alexandria

St. Croix Valley

Twin Cities Breweries

Southern Minnesota Tastings

Wine & Beer Tours
NEXT LEFT

*T*hey say there's nothing better for quenching a powerful thirst than water, but then again the folks who say that probably never had one of Minnesota's home-brewed ales in a frosty mug.

Many of the state's award-winning wines began as winter-hardy grapes. Tour the breweries and vineyards in this chapter, then taste their offerings and you'll know why Minnesota is a winner in both industries.

Alexandria

To get to Alexandria, take I-94 west of the Twin Cities (120 miles).

Carlos Creek Winery/Alexandria Farms

3 miles north of Alexandria. Take Hwy 29 north to Co 42. Stay left at the Co 42 split. Next split stay left and follow Co 34. Winery located on Co 34. 320-846-5443. www.carloscreekwinery.com.

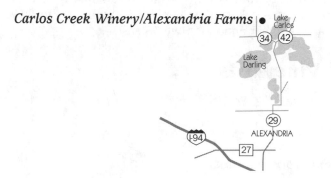

Carlos Creek Winery/Alexandria Farms

Twenty acres of grapevines and 7,000 apple trees make Carlos Creek Winery the state's largest orchard and vineyard. World recognized, award-winning wines fermented and bottled on the property. Carlos Creek/Alexandria Farms is also one of Minnesota's largest purebred Arabian horse facilities. Open year-round. Daily tours and wine tasting. Fall grape-stomping contest.

Options: Alexandria considers itself to be the "birthplace of America," claiming the Vikings explored Minnesota long before Columbus made his voyage. The proof is in the Runestone—a rock found in a nearby field, allegedly dating to 1362 and inscribed by Vikings. See the famous stone, the tooth of a woolly mammoth and much more at the **Kensington Runestone Museum**, 206 Broadway. 320-763-3160. Open daily year-round. Fee charged. • Have your picture taken with **Big Ole**, the 28', 4-ton Viking greeter as you enter town. • **Inspiration Peak**, off Co 5, north of nearby Brandon. Panoramic views from 1,750'—the highest point in western Minnesota. • Explore the 1889 **Phelps Mill**, one of the most photographed sites in the state. Park includes flour mill, millpond and stream—a great spot for a picnic or relaxing with a book. Fifteen miles east of Fergus Falls off Hwy 1. 218-736-6038. • Directly south of Alexandria, in nearby Glenwood, you'll find **Mike's**, the largest lutefisk producer in the world. The only way to learn to speak proper Minnesotan is to eat large helpings of this lye-soaked codfish—maybe not. But you can start with a tour of the business and store. 800-950-4755 • Visit the boyhood home of Nobel Prize novelist **Sinclair Lewis**. The gray clapboard building retains much of the Lewis family furniture. 810 Sinclair Lewis Ave, Sauk Center (near downtown). 320-352-5201. Open daily Memorial Day–Labor Day. Fee charged. • **Sinclair Lewis Interpretive Center**, Hwy 71 and I-94, Sauk Center (southeast of Alexandria). 320-352-5201. Lewis memorabilia and photos. Open daily Memorial Day–Labor Day. Open M–F the rest of the year. Free.

St. Croix Valley

These attractions begin in Stillwater and end just a few miles south of Hastings. From the Twin Cities, take a 20-minute drive east on I-94 to Hwy 95 north into Stillwater. Another option is Hwy 36 east.

Saint Croix Vineyards

6428 Manning Ave.; 651-430-3310; www.scvwines.com

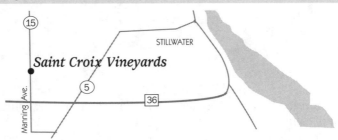

Minnesota's winter-hardy grapes produce award-winning wines. The Saint Croix Vineyards, located at Aamodt's Apple Farm, is 3 miles west of Stillwater on Manning Ave off of Hwy 36. Sample their Raspberry Infusion, Frontenac, or any of their other vintages offered at the on-site tasting room/winery. See if you don't agree that Minnesota knows good wine. May–Jul: open F–Su; Aug–Dec: open daily.

NOTE: Aamodt's also provides hot air balloon rides for a fee. See more on pg. 131.

Northern Vineyards

223 N Main St, Stillwater; 651-430-1032; www.northernvineyards.com

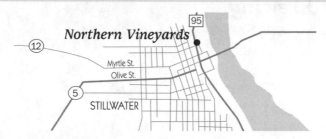

Visit Northern Vineyards' winery and tasting room. This cooperative is owned and operated by the Minnesota Wine Growers. It produces a wide selection of local wines. Tours are Saturday at 1 p.m. or by appt. Open daily.

> **Option:** Don't worry, beer lovers, you haven't been forgotten. The **Gasthaus Bavarian Hunter Restaurant** serves award-winning German cuisine and imported beer from Munich. And for a special treat, stop in on a Friday evening or Sunday afternoon for toe-tapping live accordion music. Open daily. 8390 Lofton Ave, Stillwater. 651-439-7128.

NOTE: For more things to do in Stillwater, see the Romantic Getaway chapter on pg. 131.

Alexis Bailly Vineyard

18200 Kirby Ave.; vineyard is 1 mile south of Hastings off Hwy 61 at 170th St; watch for signs. 651-437-1413; www.abvwines.com.

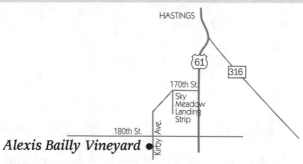

Alexis Bailly Vineyard produces nine wines with a label that reads: Minnesota: Where the grapes can suffer. Tastings offered Jun–Nov, F–Su.

NOTE: For more to see and do in Hastings, see Waterfalls chapter, pg. 188.

Twin Cities Breweries

Summit Brewing

910 Montreal Circle, St. Paul; 651-265-7800; www.summitbrewing.com

Established in 1986, Summit Brewing began life in an old auto parts warehouse and grew into a brand new facility in 1998. And no matter what fine Minnesota watering hole you saunter into, you're going to find yourself face-to-face with a Summit beer. So go ahead, order a round and you'll see why this brewery's beverage is a staple on the beer list. As founder Mark Stutrud says, "We only brew what we love to drink. Whatever's left over, we sell." Year round brewery tours Tu, Th, & Sa. Free admission; call or email for Saturday tour reservations.

Vine Park Brewing

1254 W 7th Street, St. Paul; 651-228-1355; www.vinepark.com

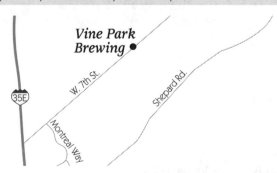

Vine Park is the state's only Brew-On-Premise (BOP) brewery and as a 10-year-old, it is also one of the oldest and most successful BOPs in the nation. All good news for those do-it-yourself brew masters who don't want the fuss, muss, and expense involved with home brewing. Vine Park Brewing provides the recipes, the ingredients, the equipment, the knowledge, and the beer coach. You provide yourself, about two hours of time, and the $125.00 it takes to brew one batch of beer which yields about 72 22-oz. bottles (plus a $45 bottle deposit). This is a great hands-on opportunity to create your own special ale. Reservations taken M–Sa.

NOTE: Wine making also available. Price ranges from $125–$145, plus $70 for bottles. Vine Park is not an eatery or bar.

Southern Minnesota Tastings

New Ulm is approximately 90 miles from the Twin Cities. Follow Hwy 169 south to St. Peter; take Co 99 to Nicollet; then Hwy 14 west.

August Schell Brewery

New Ulm. 1860 Schell Rd. South on Broadway, turn west on 18th St S, follow the signs; 507-354-5528 or 800-770-5020; www.schellsbrewery.com

Where can you go to get a good Wiener Schnitzel and a hearty German beer to wash it down with? New Ulm, of course.

The August Schell Brewery opened in 1860. Currently operated by the fifth generation, Schell's is the second-oldest, family-owned brewery in the nation. Grounds include a deer park and beautiful gardens with strutting peacocks. The charming red brick house is off-limits, as it is the residence of fourth generation Schells. Brewery tours offered Memorial Day–Labor Day, M–F. Small fee charged. Grounds and museum/gift shop open daily. Free.

Morgan Creek Vineyards

23707 478th Ave, New Ulm, MN 56073; 507-947-3547.
www.morgancreekvineyards.com. From New Ulm, take Hwy 68 roughly 10 miles
east toward Mankato; watch for sign. Turn right on Co 47, go for 2 miles, take left
on Co 101. First place on left. Use second entrance.

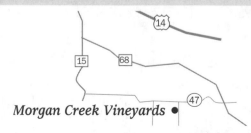

Morgan Creek Vineyards ●

Maybe you're not as German as you'd like to be and find beer a bit too
robust for the palate? Then take a trip to Morgan Creek Vineyards for some
wine instead. Seasonal events for the entire family include a Grape Stomp
Festival the first Saturday in Oct. Tours and tastings May–Dec, F–Su.

> **Option:** While you're in town, be sure to see the **New Ulm
> Glockenspiel**. This freestanding carillon clock tower chimes on the hour.
> Time your visit for either noon, 3, or 5 and watch animated figures move
> to the programmed music of the bells. Located downtown on the corner
> of Minnesota St and N 4th. For more information about New Ulm, visit
> their website: www.newulm.com or call 888-4NEWULM (888-463-9856).

The Country Pub's Wine Cafe

301 N Riverfront, Mankato; 507-345-1516.

The Country Pub's Wine Cafe

Driving eastward on Hwy 14 to Mankato, the Wine Cafe Pub & Eatery
serves over 100 wines by the glass, as well as specialty coffee and espres-
so. Open M–Sa. $–$$

> **Options:** Mankato has more than 30 parks, offering anything from fishing
> to mountain biking. www.ci.mankato.mn.us/parks/index.php3. But for the

romantic, stop in at **Minneopa State Park**. Built in 1864, this park has a picturesque double waterfall and an old stone windmill. Located 5 miles west of Mankato at the junction of Hwys 68 & 169. Follow signs. 507-389-5464 or www.dnr.state.mn.us/state_parks/minneopa/index.html; State Park permit required. • Free petting zoo, flower gardens, and a fountain are a few of the things you'll see at **Sibley Park**. It also has a beach area, camping, fishing, canoeing, baseball fields and basketball courts. Sledding and ice skating in the winter. Located off S Riverfront Dr. • **Mankato Mdewakanton Powwow**—Native Americans from across the country return to their ceremonial grounds in Land of Memories Park. Colorful costumes, traditional foods, crafts and ceremonial dancing. Mid-Sept. Park located across the river from Sibley Park. Call the Mankato Area Chamber & Convention Bureau for more information. 800-657-4733 or 507-345-4519. www.greatermankato.com. • **Mount Kato Ski & Bike** has 19 trails, 8 chair lifts, a 2-level chalet, full service rental shop and more. Also 7 miles of mountain bike trails—80% is wooded single track. Located 1 mile south of Mankato. take Hwy 66 south. Follow signs. 507-625-3363. www.mountkato.com • Mid-Jul to mid-Aug watch the **Minnesota Vikings** get in shape for the upcoming season at their Mankato training camp. Minnesota State University, Blakeslee Field. Practices held twice a day, 6 days a week. Free. Fee charged for scrimmages. www.vikings.com/home.html • Mankato also has an extensive **performing arts** theater schedule. Call Mankato Area Chamber & Convention Bureau: 800-657-4733 or 507-345-4519; www.greatermankato.com.

August Schell Brewery (pg. 197)

Scenic Byways

Waters of the Dancing Sky

Gunflint Trail

Avenue of Pines

Scenic Highway

Edge of the Wilderness

North Shore

Great River Road

Skyline Parkway

Lake Country

Paul Bunyan

Rushing Rapids

Otter Trail

Veterans Evergreen Memorial

Glacial Ridge Trail

Grand Rounds

Great River Road

Minnesota River Valley

Apple Blossom Drive

Historic Bluff Country

Shooting Star

THEME: ODDS & ENDS

Haunted Minnesota

The Lost Forty

Scenic Byways

Sports

Winter Fun

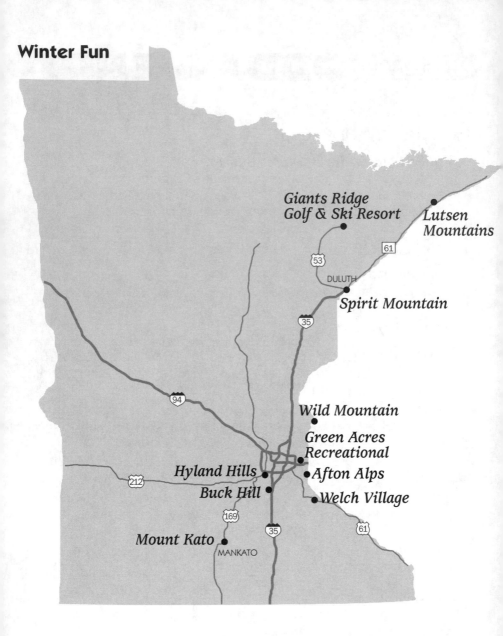

Giants Ridge
Golf & Ski Resort

Lutsen
Mountains

61

53

DULUTH

Spirit Mountain

35

94

Wild Mountain

Green Acres
Recreational

Hyland Hills

212

Afton Alps

Buck Hill

Welch Village

169

35

61

Mount Kato

MANKATO

*H*ere's tons of useful information not available through the theme chapters. Names, addresses, websites and phone numbers for everything from haunted buildings to sporting events.

Haunted Minnesota

There's only one thing better than sitting around a campfire telling ghost stories, and that's actually exploring Minnesota's own haunted sites.

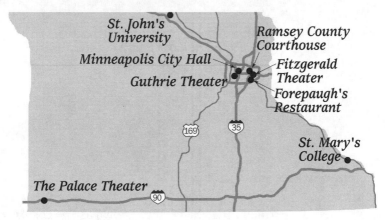

Public Places with Resident Ghosts

Fitzgerald Theater: 10 E Exchange St, St. Paul, MN. 651-290-1221. www.fitzgeraldtheater.org. Two ghosts.

Forepaugh's Restaurant: 276 S Exchange St, St. Paul, MN. 651-224-5606. www.forepaughs.com. At least one ghost.

Guthrie Theater: 818 S 2nd St, Minneapolis, MN. 612-377-2224 or 877-447-8243. www.guthrietheater.org. At least one ghost.

Minneapolis City Hall: 350 S 5th St, Minneapolis, MN. 612-673-2363. At least one ghost.

NOTE: The City Hall Carillon Committee holds bell concerts regularly at the Minneapolis City Hall. Call 612-673-5311 for concert schedule. Free.

The Palace Theater: 104 E Main and N Freeman, Luverne, MN. www.palacetheater.us. Two ghosts.

Ramsey County Courthouse: 15 W Kellogg Blvd, St. Paul, MN. 651-266-8350. www.co.ramsey.mn.us. Multiple ghosts.

St. John's University: P.O. Box 2000, Collegeville, MN. 320-363-2011. www.csbsju.edu. Multiple ghosts.

St. Mary's College: 700 Terrace Heights, Winona, MN. 507-452-4430 or 800-635-5987. One nasty ghost.

The Lost Forty

From Bemidji, take Hwy 71 north to Co 30 east (which turns into Co 13). At the T, turn left onto Hwy 46 (north), then east on Co 29; turn north onto Co 26.

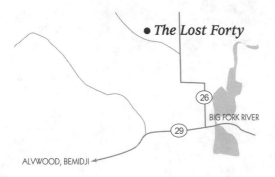

Minnesota has its own Bermuda Triangle of sorts, known as The Lost Forty. This is 40 acres of virgin forest, originally missing from the state's tally of total acreage.

You'll find The Lost Forty in the Chippewa National Forest, approximately 50 miles northeast of Bemidji. Picturesque hiking trails through mature white pines, maples and oaks.

> **Option:** Since you're in the neighborhood, stop in at **Hafeman Boat Works** to watch the nearly lost art of birch bark canoe making. Ray Boessel Jr. constructs canoes ranging in size from 5–26' long, turning out one per week during the summer months. His wife's grandfather started the business in 1921. Located at 59520 Hwy 6, Bigfork. 218-743-3709.

Scenic Byways

To help you find those great views, Minnesota designated over 2,000 miles of roads as scenic byways. For more information, call the Minnesota Office of Tourism at 800-657-3700 or 651-296-5029. www.exploreminnesota.com. 500 Metro Square, 121 Seventh Pl E, Suite 100, St. Paul, MN 55101. See map on pg. 210.

North/Central West

Waters of the Dancing Sky: 191 miles. Named for the shimmering northern lights, this is the state's northernmost byway. Following Hwy 11 from Karlstad to International Falls, travel this route of lakes, woods, small towns and farmland.

Scenic Highway: 28 miles. Cut through the western side of the Chippewa National Forest on Hwy 39 from Blackduck to Cass Lake. A blend of pine, aspen and birch forests, lakes, wetlands, hayfields and bogs.

Lake Country: 88 miles. This Northwoods drive takes in the lake country between Detroit Lakes and Walker on Hwy 34, with a short jaunt north from Park Rapids to Itasca State Park on Hwy 71. Lots of pine/hardwood forests and numerous lakes interspersed with some farmland.

Otter Trail: 150 miles. A circular route through rolling hills thick with maple, oak, birch and more than 1,000 lakes. Very colorful fall drive. Fergus Falls area.

Paul Bunyan: 48 miles. According to one Paul Bunyan tall tale, the puddles left behind by the giant lumberjack's footprints became Minnesota's 10,000 lakes. Two loops on country roads explore the area north of Brainerd.

Northeast

Avenue of Pines: 46 miles. Largely undeveloped, this rustic, paved road carves through lakes, marshes and a pine forest. It also crosses the Laurentian Divide, the point separating the waters that flow north to Hudson Bay and south into the Mississippi. Route travels Hwy 46 from Deer River to Northome.

Edge of the Wilderness: 46 miles. From Grand Rapids to Effie on Hwy 38, you'll explore a region thick with lakes and the Chippewa National Forest—home to the largest population of Bald Eagles in the continental U.S.

Gunflint Trail: 57 miles. Hwy 12 travels from the scenic harbor town of Grand Marais inland through the rolling hills of Superior National Forest. The Gunflint Trail borders the Boundary Waters Canoe Area Wilderness. Besides bird watching, this road is a great place to see deer, moose, bear and wolves.

North Shore: 154 miles. From Duluth to the Canadian border, travel scenic Hwy 61 along Lake Superior for lighthouses, eight state parks with tons of waterfalls and hiking, giant ore freighters, historical towns, fish boils, a reconstruction of a late-1700s fur-trading post and so much more.

Skyline Parkway: 38 miles. Follow a ridge line high above Duluth for breathtaking views of Lake Superior and the Duluth harbor.

Rushing Rapids: 9 miles. This short, awe-inspiring drive on Hwy 210 winds along the St. Louis River through Jay Cooke State Park. Incredible view of the gorge from a swinging suspension bridge.

Veterans Evergreen Memorial: 50 miles. Hwy 23 from Askov to Duluth is a mix of farmland and woods, crisscrossed by meandering creeks. Great fall colors.

Twin Cities

Grand Rounds: 53 miles. The only urban national scenic byway, Grand Rounds follows parkways in a loop through Minneapolis, skirting the chain of lakes on the west side. See the famous Stone Arch Bridge and Minnehaha Falls.

South

Glacial Ridge Trail: 220 miles. From Willmar to Alexandria, explore a rolling terrain of lakes, woodlands and farmland.

Minnesota River Valley: 300 miles. From Belle Plaine, the Minnesota River Valley dips south to Mankato before heading northwest to Browns Valley. Take in some of the state's best farmland, as well as the world's oldest rock (3.5 billion years).

Apple Blossom Drive: 19 miles. Travel a loop south off of Hwy 61 through the Richard J. Dorer Memorial Hardwood Forest down to La Crescent—the Apple Capital of Minnesota. Numerous bluff orchards with spring apple blossoms and brilliant fall color.

Historic Bluff Country: 88 miles. Hwy 16 heading west from La Crescent to Dexter offers sweeping views, picture-perfect trout streams, limestone cliffs, Forestville/Mystery Cave State Park and charming villages.

Shooting Star: 28 miles. Travel Hwy 56 from the Iowa border heading northwest through Lake Louise State Park, over to Rose Creek. This is prairie and wildflower country much as it was when the first settlers came to the region.

All Regions

Great River Road: 562 miles. The Great River Road follows the Mississippi River from its birthplace at Itasca State Park, winding all the way south to the Iowa border. Many quaint and interesting river towns along this route including Aitkin, Little Falls, Monticello, Hastings, Red Wing, Wabasha and Winona.

Sports

Call the numbers listed below for game schedule and ticket information.

Minnesota Thunder Soccer

Minnesota Timberwolves &
Minnesota Lynx Basketball

University of Minnesota Athletics

Minnesota Twins Baseball &
Minnesota Vikings Football

St. Paul Saints Baseball

Minnesota Wild Hockey

Canterbury Park

Minnesota Wild NHL Hockey: 651-222-WILD (651-222-9453); Xcel Energy Center, 175 W Kellogg Blvd, St. Paul, MN 55102; www.wild.com

Minnesota Timberwolves Basketball: 612-989-5151 or 612-337-DUNK (612-337-3865); Target Center, 601 1st Ave N, Minneapolis; www.nba.com/timberwolves

Minnesota Lynx WNBA Basketball: 612-673-8400 or 612-337-3865; Target Center, 601 1st Ave N, Minneapolis; www.wnba.com/lynx

Minnesota Twins Baseball: 612-33TWINS (612-338-9467) or 800-33TWINS (800-338-9467); HHH Metrodome. Downtown Minneapolis; www.twinsbaseball.com

Minnesota Vikings Football: 612-338-4537; HHH Metrodome. Downtown Minneapolis; www.vikings.com

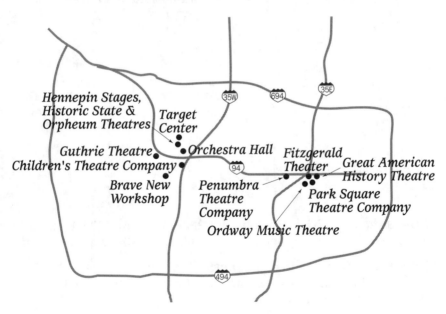

St. Paul Saints Baseball: 651-644-6659; Midway Stadium, St. Paul; www.saintsbaseball.com

Minnesota Thunder Soccer: 651-917-TEAM (8326); www.mnthunder.com

University of Minnesota Athletics: 612-624-8080 or 800-UGOPHER (800-846-7437); University of Minnesota Twin Cities' Campus.

Canterbury Park (Horse Racing): 952-445-RACE (952-445-7223) or 800-340-6361; 1100 Canterbury Rd, Shakopee; www.canterburypark.com

Twin Cities Theater & Music

Minnesota is second only to New York in the number of theaters per capita. Check with the theater listed for shows, times and tickets.

Brave New Workshop: 2605 Hennepin Ave S, Minneapolis. 612-332-6620. www.bravenewworkshop.com. Comedy and satire performances year-round.

Chanhassen Dinner Theatre: 501 W 78th St, Chanhassen; 952-934-1525. www.chanhassentheatres.com. Largest professional dinner theater in the country with performances year-round. Wheelchair accessible.

Children's Theatre Company: 2400 3rd Ave S, Minneapolis. 612-874-0400. www.childrenstheatre.org. Wheelchair accessible.

Fitzgerald Theater: 10 E Exchange St (Exchange and Wabasha Sts), St. Paul. 651-290-1221. www. fitzgeraldtheater.publicradio.org. Home of A Prairie Home Companion radio show. Full schedule of concerts and performances.

Great American History Theatre: 30 E 10th St, St. Paul. 651-292-4323. www.historytheatre.com. Performances Sep–May. Wheelchair accessible.

Guthrie Theater: 818 S 2nd St, Minneapolis. 612-377-2224 or 877-447-8243. www.guthrietheater.org. Performances year-round. Wheelchair accessible.

Hennepin Stages: 824 Hennepin Ave, Minneapolis. 612-373-5600. www.hennepintheatredistrict.org. Performances year-round. Wheelchair accessible.

Historic State and Orpheum Theatres: Hennepin Ave between 9th and 10th St S, Minneapolis; 612-373-5600. www.hennepintheatredistrict.org. Broadway touring shows and variety of concerts. Wheelchair accessible.

Orchestra Hall: Nicollet Mall at 11th St, Minneapolis. 612-371-5656. www.minnesotaorchestra.org. Home to Minnesota Orchestra. Wheelchair accessible.

Ordway Music Theatre: 345 Washington St, St. Paul. 651-224-4222. www.orway.org. Home to the St. Paul Chamber Orchestra and Minnesota Opera, with full schedule of other concerts and touring shows. Wheelchair accessible.

Park Square Theatre Company: 20 W 7th Place, St. Paul. 651-291-7005. www.parksquaretheatre.org. Performances Jan–Aug; Wheelchair accessible.

Penumbra Theatre Company: 270 N Kent St, St. Paul. 651-224-3180. www.penumbratheatre.org. The only professional black theater group in Minnesota. Presents the Black Nativity each holiday season as well as August Wilson plays.

Target Center: 600 1st Ave N, Minneapolis; 612-673-0900. Concerts, performances and sporting events including Timberwolves and Lynx basketball. www.targetcenter.com. Wheelchair accessible.

Winter Fun

One of the best things about Minnesota is the changing seasons. As the saying goes, "If you don't like the weather we're having now, wait one minute."

Winter brings new opportunities for fun and adventure. The parks system offers sliding, snowshoeing, cross-country skiing, ice skating and snowmobiling. Over 10,000 frozen lakes provide great ice fishing. Pick up snowmobile trail maps at information centers or rural area businesses. See map on pg. 202.

Downhill Skiing

Buck Hill: Located off I-35 in Burnsville. 952-435-7174. Chalet, 8 lifts, 16 runs. www.buckhill.com.

Hyland Hills: 8800 Chalet Rd, Bloomington. 763-694-7800. www.hylandski.com. Chalet, 3 lifts, 12 runs.

Giants Ridge Golf & Ski Resort: Biwabik. 877-442-6877 or 218-865-3000. www.giantsridge.com. 35 alpine runs, 60 km groomed cross-country ski trails, access to more than 2,000 miles of groomed snowmobile trails, resort lodging, entertainment, 18-hole golf course.

Afton Alps: 6600 Peller Ave S, Hastings (15 miles east of St. Paul). 800-328-1328 or 651-436-5245. 5 chalets, 18 lifts, 48 runs. www.aftonalps.com

Wild Mountain: Hwy 16, Taylors Falls. 800-447-4958 or 651-465-6315. www.wildmountain.com. Chalet, 4 lifts, 23 runs.

Welch Village: South of the Metro. Take the Welch Village Road from Hwy 61. 651-258-4567. www.welchvillage.com. 2 chalets, 8 lifts, 50 runs.

Mount Kato: Located 1 mile south of Mankato, off Hwy 66 S. 800-668-5286 or 507-625-3363. www.mountkato.com. Chalet, 8 lifts, 3 handle tows, 19 runs.

Spirit Mountain: 9500 Spirit Mountain Pl, Duluth. 800-642-6377. www.spiritmt.com. Chalet, 5 lifts, 22 runs (700' vertical drop).

Lutsen Mountains: 467 Ski Hill Rd, Lutsen. 218-663-7281. www.lutsen.com. 85 mountain runs (800' vertical drop), chalet, restaurant, resort lodging, summer hiking, horseback riding and the Alpine Slide—a half-mile scream of a ride on a plastic sled. Lutsen has one of the Midwest's only gondola rides.

Snow Tubing

Green Acres Recreational: 8989 N 55th St, Lake Elmo (off Hwy 36). 651-770-6060. www.greenacresrec.com. Chalet with concessions, 2 hills, 3 rope tows. Inner tubes provided. Call or check website for hours.

Index

218